GOSPEL FOUNDATIONS

THE KINGDOM ON EARTH
VOL. 6 | Acts–Revelation

6

From the creators of *The Gospel Project*, *Gospel Foundations* is a six-volume resource that teaches the storyline of Scripture. It is comprehensive in scope yet concise enough to be completed in just one year. Each seven-session volume includes videos to help your group understand the way each text fits into the storyline of the Bible.

© 2018 LifeWay Press®

No part of this work may be reproduced or transmitted in any form or by any means, electronic or mechanical, including photocopying and recording, or by any information storage or retrieval system, except as may be expressly permitted in writing by the publisher. Requests for permission should be addressed in writing to LifeWay Press®; One LifeWay Plaza; Nashville, TN 37234.

ISBN 9781535915564 • Item 005805891

Dewey decimal classification: 230

Subject headings: CHRISTIANITY / GOSPEL / SALVATION

EDITORIAL TEAM

Ben Trueblood
Director, Student Ministry

JohnPaul Basham
Manager, Student Ministry Publishing

Andy McLean
Content Editor

Grace Pepper
Production Editor

Alli Quattlebaum
Graphic Designer

We believe that the Bible has God for its author; salvation for its end; and truth, without any mixture of error, for its matter and that all Scripture is totally true and trustworthy. To review LifeWay's doctrinal guideline, please visit lifeway.com/doctrinalguideline.

Scripture quotations are taken from the Christian Standard Bible®, Copyright © 2017 by Holman Bible Publishers. Used by permission.

Christian Standard Bible® and CSB® are federally registered trademarks of Holman Bible Publishers.

To order additional copies of this resource, write to LifeWay Resources Customer Service; One LifeWay Plaza; Nashville, TN 37234; fax 615-251-5933; call toll free 800-458-2772; order online at LifeWay.com; email orderentry@lifeway.com; or visit the LifeWay Christian Store serving you.

Printed in the United States of America

Student Ministry Publishing
LifeWay Resources
One LifeWay Plaza
Nashville, TN 37234

CONTENTS

ABOUT *THE GOSPEL PROJECT*

Gospel Foundations is from the creators of *The Gospel Project*, which exists to point kids, students, and adults to the gospel of Jesus Christ through weekly group Bible studies and additional resources that show how God's plan of redemption unfolds throughout Scripture and still today, compelling them to join the mission of God.

The Gospel Project provides theological yet practical, age-appropriate Bible studies that immerse your entire church in the story of the gospel, helping to develop a gospel culture that leads to gospel mission:

Gospel Story

Immersing people of all ages in the storyline of Scripture: God's plan to rescue and redeem His creation through His Son, Jesus Christ.

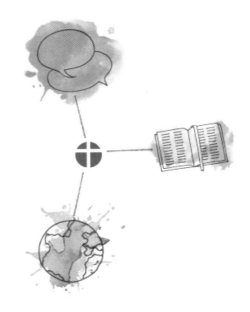

Gospel Culture

Inspiring communities where the gospel saturates our experience and doubters become believers who become declarers of the gospel.

Gospel Mission

Empowering believers to live on mission, declaring the good news of the gospel in word and deed.

HOW TO USE THIS STUDY

This Bible-study book includes seven weeks of content for group and personal study. Each session is divided into the following components:

Introduction

Every session contains an intro option for your group time, allowing there to be a natural transition into the material for that week.

Setting the Context

This section is designed to provide the context to the biblical passage being discussed. It will help group members to not only better understand the passage under consideration for each session, but also how the biblical storyline connects between each session. It is also in this section that you will find the reference to the informational graphic for each session, once again helping students to have a deeper understanding into the storyline of Scripture.

Session Videos

Each session has a corresponding video to help tell the Bible story. After watching the video, spend some time discussing the questions provided, as well any additional questions raised by your students in response to the video.

Group Discussion

After watching the video, continue the group discussion by reading the Scripture passages and discussing the questions on these pages. Additional content is also provided on these pages to grant additional clarity into the meaning of these passages. In addition, it is in this section that you find the Christ Connection, showing students how all of Scripture points to Jesus.

Head, Heart, Hands

This section is designed to close out your group time by personally reflecting on how God's Story challenges the way we think, feel, and live as a result. Because God's Word is capable of changing everything about a person, this section seeks to spell out how each session is able to transform our Heads, Hearts, and Hands.

Personal Study

Five personal devotions are provided for each session to take individuals deeper into Scripture and to supplement the content introduced in the group study. With biblical teaching and introspective questions, these sections challenge individuals to grow in their understanding of God's Word and to respond in faith.

GOD'S WORD TO YOU

"And they all lived happily ever after."

This is the coda, the postscript that punctuates the tales of our childhoods. The prince is victorious. The dragon is defeated. The princess is rescued. The struggle is over. The battle is won. And finally, "they all lived happily ever after."

The Bible has its coda as well. But unlike the happily-ever-afters of fairy tales, this is one of expectation—not for the end to come but for the next chapter to be written. A promise summarized in three words: "Come, Lord Jesus" (Rev. 22:20). This is the promise the entire story of Scripture builds toward. It is the deepest longing of the heart of God's people. The first man and woman longed for the coming of the Son, the One whose heel would crush the head of the serpent (Gen. 3:15). Abraham longed for the promised Offspring through whom all nations would be blessed (Gen. 12:3,7). David longed to see his Lord, the Son who would sit on the throne of an unfading kingdom (Ps. 110:1). God's people—in exile and return—longed for the coming of the Servant who would restore them (Isa. 49:6-7).

Then the long-expected One came—Jesus, the Son of David, the Son of Abraham, the Son of Eve, the Son of God—bringing redemption and peace with God by humbling Himself to the point of death and then being exalted in His resurrection (Phil. 2:8-11).

News of the reconciliation Jesus offered spread throughout the world. People of every tribe and tongue and nation believed and trusted Christ for the forgiveness of their sins. And as this good news continued to spread, the promise spread with it—the promise that tells of the day when Jesus returns to make all things new. When every tear will be wiped from every eye. When suffering, sadness, and death will be no more. In their place will be joy, gladness, and life everlasting as God dwells with His people forevermore.

But for now, we wait. And as we do, we join with our brothers and sisters across the centuries as we long for that day to come, echoing these words: "Amen! Come, Lord Jesus!"

THE SPIRIT COMES

GOD CALLS US TO RELY ON THE HOLY SPIRIT AS WE SHARE THE GOSPEL.

INTRODUCTION

▶ What is the best gift you have ever received (outside of salvation)? Who gave it to you? What made it so special? What was the occasion?

Gifts are powerful things. A gift, given genuinely and lovingly, is a way of making or affirming a bond. They are like punctuation marks on relationships. When a gift is given without asking for anything in return, without any sense of obligation, it's a powerful thing.

The gospel is the free gift of grace from God: foreshadowed in the Old Testament, revealed first in the stories of the Gospels, and then proclaimed and expounded upon throughout the Book of Acts and the rest of the New Testament (Rom. 6:23).

The gospel not only comes from God but is also spread by God's own handiwork. The Book of Acts communicates the spread of the gospel to all people through the apostles and the churches they planted (Acts 1:8). However, the primary Actor in the Book of Acts—spreading the gospel, building up the church, and healing the sick—is God Himself. More specifically, God in the person of the Holy Spirit who gave gifts of life and redemption to advance God's kingdom.

SETTING THE CONTEXT

Jesus continued to instruct and encourage His disciples for forty days after His resurrection. Then, just before He ascended into heaven, Jesus clarified the mission He was giving them. The disciples were to be Jesus' witnesses; they were to tell others about who He is and what He has done to provide salvation to the world. And this mission would take them to the ends of the earth, to every nation, tongue, and tribe. But first, they were to wait in Jerusalem for the Father's promise.

So they waited together for ten days, united in prayer, until the day of Pentecost. But this Pentecost celebration would be like none other. It was during this Pentecost that Jesus' disciples would experience the provision of the Holy Spirit. The Book of Acts tells of the wonderful works of the Holy Spirit through Jesus' disciples. "Hearing the Old Testament in Acts" (p. 10) shows how even these events were foretold by God.

HEARING THE
OLD TESTAMENT *IN* ACTS

OLD TESTAMENT	*NEW TESTAMENT*
The Tower of Babylon God Confused Humanity with Different Languages (Gen. 11:1-9)	**Pentacost** The Filling with the Holy Spirit Overcame Language Barriers (Acts 2:1-13)
The Promise of the Spirit God Will Pour Out His Spirit on All Humanity (Joel 2:28-32)	**The Outpouring of the Spirit** The Promise of the Spirit Fulfilled (Acts 2:14-21)
Opposition to the Messiah The Nations Plot in Vain Against the Lord's Anointed (Ps. 2)	**Opposition to the Church** The Messiah's People Prayed for Boldness (Acts 4:23-31)
The LORD Called and Sent Prophets for His Name to His People and the Nations (Jer. 1; Ezek. 2)	**Jesus** Called Saul to Take His Name to Gentiles, Kings, and Israelites (Acts 9; 22; 26)
David's House The Nations That Bear God's Name Will Be Included (Amos 9:11-12)	**The Church** The Gentiles Who Are Called by Jesus' Name Are Included (Acts 15:14-19)

SESSION VIDEOS

Watch this session's video, and then continue the group discussion using the following guide.

▶ What ideas or phrases stood out to you most in the video? Why?

▶ How do Christians experience the person and work of the Holy Spirit in their lives?

GROUP DISCUSSION

As a group, read Acts 2:1-4.

⭐ How does this passage reveal both the power and the purpose of the Holy Spirit?

▶ Why is it significant that the tongues of fire rested on each believer?

After Jesus gave His final instructions to the disciples and ascended into heaven, the disciples would leave from there and spend the next ten days gathered together in an upstairs room in Jerusalem praying for the Father's promise to be fulfilled. Without warning, the Spirit rushed into the world, the room, and their hearts as He manifested Himself in what appeared like flickering flames resting on each person there.

In the Spirit's coming, Jesus' promise to always be with us makes sense, as does the prophet Joel's promise that God would one day pour out His Spirit on all people (Joel 2:28). When we respond to the gospel with faith in Jesus, we receive this extraordinary gift—the promised Holy Spirit. The Spirit brings gives us the power to participate in God's redeeming work, as well as the assurance that we are never alone in this work. The promise of Immanuel, "God with us," was fulfilled in Jesus (Matt 1:23), who took on flesh and walked among us, and His Holy Spirit is with us and in us, even to the end of the age.

▶ How would you have responded if you had seen what happened at Pentecost?

▶ In what way does the Spirit enabling the believers that day give you confidence to do what God has called you to do?

GROUP DISCUSSION *CONT.*

As a group, read Acts 2:22-24,36-40.

▶ What are the essential components of sharing the gospel based on this section of Peter's sermon?

★ Why is it important that Peter gave the people a way to respond?

▶ In what ways might we complicate the gospel as we share it?

It didn't take long after the Holy Spirit's arrival for Him to reveal His great passion and purpose. The sound of the rushing wind caught the attention of a great crowd of Jews who were in Jerusalem for the festival of Pentecost. These Jews from every nation gathered together to investigate and heard the good news of Jesus—each in their own language, as the Spirit enabled the disciples to speak in different languages. Filled with the Spirit, the Apostle Peter responded to the crowd's confusion as he stood before them and preached this sermon.

As a group, read Acts 2:41-47.

▶ What activities did the church engage in? Why was each vital?

★ What does it mean that the early church was filled with awe of God? How might this relate to "the fear of the Lord"?

▶ Do we have that same fear of God today? Why or why not?

This passage mentions many signs of God's grace and God's work. Wonders and signs referred to miracles such as healing the sick and casting out demons, which characterized both Jesus' ministry and the apostles' ministry; however, more subtle miracles occurred as well. These believers shared their possessions, sold whatever extra they had in order to give away the proceeds to those in need among them, and met regularly and shared meals.

This kind of abundant, intense, and dedicated community life should be seen for the miracle it is. This kind of living doesn't just happen. When you force people to live in small, shared spaces, usually the opposite occurs. Closeness leads to conflicts, and conflicts lead to strengthened borders. In Acts 2, this newly formed community pressed into one another's lives and the boundaries around possessions and wealth disappeared. As believers were moved by the Spirit, their interests shifted from self to the good of the community of faith.

When the Holy Spirit takes up residence in our hearts, we begin to overflow with love for God and love for our neighbors, especially those who share our faith. These twin loves for God and others fuel the whole of the Christian life. Love of God leads us to bear witness to the gospel around the world, and love of our brothers and sisters leads us to develop rich, deeply committed relationships with God's people.

CHRIST CONNECTION

Jesus had instructed His disciples to wait for the Holy Spirit because the Spirit would empower them to be His witnesses on earth. Just as Jesus had promised, the Holy Spirit came upon the disciples, filled them, and empowered them at Pentecost, resulting in three thousand new believers. God gives the Holy Spirit to those who trust in Jesus as Lord and Savior, and the Spirit changes us to be more like Jesus.

OUR MISSION

Head

What thoughts or expectations do you have about believers being filled with the Holy Spirit?

How would you explain the importance of the Spirit's presence in believers' lives?

Heart

Read Ephesians 5:18-19 and Acts 13:50-52. What stands out most to you about these passages?

How should the indwelling of the Spirit change the way believers live?

Hands

What are some obstacles that might prevent people from experiencing true community? Why do you think we sometimes struggle with overcoming these obstacles?

What are some ways we can contribute to this Spirit-filled community of faith?

PERSONAL STUDY: DAY 1

⭐ **The point: Isaiah prophesied about the coming of the Holy Spirit.**

▶ Read Isaiah 11:2.

Highlight the word **"him."** Who was this referring to? How do you know?

What attributes of the Spirit are listed? How will these characteristics make this King different from other kings?

Think about the word **"rest"** used in this verse. What does the use of the word **"rest"** tell you about the relationship between the King and the Spirit of the Lord?

▶ Respond

Review the characteristics of the Spirit—wisdom, understanding, counsel, strength, knowledge, and fear of the Lord. Describe how the Spirit of the Lord has worked through you in similar ways and the result of His working in your life.

While Isaiah 11:2 details the characteristics of the Spirit of the Lord, Galatians 5:22-23 describe the characteristics we will have when we are living a Spirit-filled life. List those characteristics and write a prayer to God asking Him to help you increase in these areas.

⭐ **The point: The Holy Spirit indwells every believer.**

▶ Read Acts 2:1-4.

What did the believers do after they were filled with the Holy Spirit?

How does their experience influence your perspective on your ability to do things God may ask you to do?

Jesus had already told His disciples a Counselor was coming in John 14:16-17. In addition to what you learned about the Holy Spirit in today's passage, what do these verses teach you about Him?

▶ Respond

Jot down some of the characteristics of the Holy Spirit you have observed. Then reflect on the fact that the same Spirit that came upon the apostles at Pentecost lives inside you today. How should that affect the way you live?

Write a prayer to God asking Him to live life through the power of the Spirit so you can accomplish something He has recently asked you to do.

★ The point: Believers are the temple of the Holy Spirit.

▶ Read 1 Corinthians 6:19.

How should the Holy Spirit living inside us make us different from non-Christians?

Paul said that we are not our own because we were bought with a price (v. 20). Who paid that price and what place should He have in our lives as a result?

In 2 Corinthians 5:17, Paul says believers are new creations. Think about your own life and list some ways believers are made new.

▶ Respond

Consider what it means that your body is the temple of the Holy Spirit. How might this change how you feel about or treat your body.

In light of the fact that your body is the temple of the Holy Spirit, do you have any habits or behaviors that don't bring God glory? Say a prayer asking God to forgive you and to help you live a more Spirit-filled life.

PERSONAL STUDY: DAY 4

⭐ **The point: The Holy Spirit empowers God's people to share the gospel.**

▶ Read Acts 2:32-40.

What are some factors that caused Peter to speak so passionately?
(Hint: Focus on verses 32 and 36 and review Acts 2:4 for additional insight.)

Jesus told the apostles they would receive power when the Holy Spirit came upon them (Acts 1:8). Why would they need to be empowered to be Jesus' witnesses throughout the world?

Describe the audience's response to Peter's message and how he answered their questions.

What do you think it means to be empowered by the Spirit or compelled to speak out, like the believers in these verses were?

▶ Respond

Sometimes the thought of sharing our faith with others can seem scary. List some reasons you might be hesitant to share your faith. Then, make another list of all the reasons you should share your faith, supporting each one with Scripture.

For further study on God's love for us, read Romans 5:8; Ephesians 3:17b-19; 1 John 3:1; and 1 John 4:9,19. Start praying for the opportunity to show God's love to someone in your circle of influence this week.

PERSONAL STUDY: DAY 5

⭐ **The point: The Holy Spirit strengthens believers and builds community.**

▶ Read Acts 2:41-47.

The believers in Acts 2 experienced a unique kind of community. What were their priorities during this time?

What barriers might prevent us from experiencing this kind of community in today's world?

What made it possible for the believers in Acts 2 to live this way? What does that tell you about the power of the Spirit to work in you and in your church family or youth group?

▶ Respond

Think about your own possessions and the items you own that have meaning to you. Would you be able to give those things up for the good of someone else? Why or why not?

Review the things you've learned about the Holy Spirit this week. Choose something you didn't know before or that is especially meaningful to you and discuss it with a friend.

THE CHURCH
IS SCATTERED

*GOD CALLS US TO GLORIFY JESUS, EVEN WHEN
WE ARE PERSECUTED.*

INTRODUCTION

Have you ever heard the phrase "delayed gratification"? It is commonly understood to be the conscious choice to avoid one pleasurable thing because avoiding it will lead to greater pleasure in the long run. For example, I may stay in school for a better paying future job even though staying may not be the most fun thing to do. Maybe I wait to buy a new pair of shoes for the delayed gratification of buying a new cellphone after saving up.

▶ What are some additional examples of delayed gratification? How have you personally experienced it?

In one sense, Christians operate according to this idea of delayed gratification, especially when it comes to persecution. Why would someone endure pain and suffering? What stops them from simply denying their faith and changing their lifestyles to avoid persecution? Answer: Delayed gratification in knowing that the sufferings of this age are both light and momentary compared to the "eternal weight of glory" (2 Cor. 4:17) awaiting those who remain steadfast in their belief in Christ.

SETTING THE CONTEXT

The church was born in an extraordinary way, accompanied by the amazing signs of the Holy Spirit's arrival, a bold sermon, and thousands trusting in Christ, with more believers added to the church every day. The church in Jerusalem lived together in fellowship and grew in their faith. But this nearly ideal beginning would not last.

Before long, Peter and John healed a man who was lame and proclaimed the gospel, claiming that the healing was evidence of Jesus' resurrection and calling people to repent and believe. This was too much for the same religious aristocracy who had orchestrated the crucifixion of Jesus just weeks before. Peter and John were arrested and forbidden from speaking in the name of Jesus— the first act of persecution against the church that would soon escalate toward violence. "Suffering for Jesus" (p. 22) traces this progression of persecution against the church.

SUFFERING *FOR JESUS*

ACTS OF MINISTRY	THE FORM OF PERSECUTION	THE RESULTS
Peter, along with John, healed a lame man and then preached in Jesus' name (Acts 3:1-26)	Peter and John were arrested by the Sanhedrin and threatened if they spoke in Jesus' name again (Acts 4:3-22)	The church prayed for boldness in the face of opposition, which the Lord granted through His Holy Spirit (Acts 4:23-31)
Through the apostles, the sick and those with unclean spirits were being healed (Acts 5:12-16)	The apostles were arrested and tried by the Sanhedrin, flogged and ordered not to speak in Jesus' name (Acts 5:18-41)	The apostles rejoiced that they were counted worthy to suffer for Jesus' name and continued proclaiming the good news about Jesus (Acts 5:41-42)
Stephen performed great wonders and signs among the people and spoke with wisdom from the Holy Spirit (Acts 6:8-10; 7:1-53)	Stephen was falsely accused of blasphemy against the temple and taken outside the city and stoned to death (Acts 6:11-14; 7:57-60)	Stephen prayed for forgiveness for those stoning him (Acts 7:59-60) Persecution broke out against the church and scattered believers throughout the world preaching the word about Jesus (Acts 8:1,4; 11:19-20)

SESSION VIDEOS

Watch this session's video, and then continue the group discussion using the following guide.

▶ What ideas or phrases stood out to you most in the video? Why?

▶ What are some of the things we learn about faith under pressure from the account of Stephen?

GROUP DISCUSSION

As a group, read Acts 6:8-15.

⭐ What attributes of Stephen are evident from these verses?

▶ What are some of the ways we can and should rely on the Spirit as we tell others about the gospel?

Stephen, filled with the Holy Spirit, received a reputation for performing signs and wonders while testifying to the Jews about who Jesus is. As a result, he attracted the attention of men who wanted to argue with him. They challenged him and hoped to stop his testimony, but because he was wise and filled with the Spirit of God, their efforts fell short.

This is a consistent theme in the Book of Acts: ordinary men like Stephen and Peter taking up debates with well-educated clergy and winning. Their unfair advantage in these debates was twofold. First, they were on the side of the truth (which makes winning any debate much easier). Second, they were filled with the Holy Spirit, which gave them supernatural wisdom in what to say and when.

As the story went on, Stephen was taken before the Sanhedrin, a body of religious leaders who oversaw the Jewish community. There, his opponents resorted to low and dirty tactics, lying about what Stephen had been preaching and teaching.

▶ When has someone lied about something you said or did in order to get you in trouble? How did the false witnesses do the same to Stephen?

GROUP DISCUSSION *CONT.*

As a group, read Acts 7:44-53.

▶ What are some of the Old Testament stories that Stephen chose to reference in his defense against the Sanhedrin?

⭐ What does Stephen's use of Scripture reveal about how he viewed it?

▶ How should Stephen's charge against the Sanhedrin shape the way we share the gospel?

Stephen's sermon might sound a little odd us. In order to understand how powerful this message was and why the reaction against it was so strong, we need to keep two things in mind as we read Stephen's words.

First, to Stephen's Jewish audience, nothing on earth was as sacred as the temple. The temple in Jerusalem was the high point of all of Jewish history. Their exclusive claim as Jews was that the one true God dwelled with Israel. First, He dwelled with them when they wandered in the desert, manifesting Himself in the tabernacle they carried through the wilderness. After they conquered the promised land, Solomon commissioned a temple to be built in Jerusalem.

Second, Israel was unfaithful to their covenant with God. They turned to the gods and idols of their neighbors. Eventually, they were conquered, the temple was destroyed, and the nation was crushed. For generations, the temple was no more than rubble. The temple's reconstruction came with a revival. Its presence in Jerusalem was seen as a sign that God would be coming back to Israel and that the Israelites would one day be free from the tyranny of the nations.

As a group, read Acts 7:54-60.

▶ Why did the leaders react so violently against Stephen?

⭐ What was the purpose of Stephen's vision of Jesus standing next to God's throne?

The Sanhedrin was enraged by Stephen's sermon, especially by his charge that they had received but not kept the law. There was nothing else to hear, so they led Stephen out to have him stoned. Stephen had preached Jesus; now it was time to show Jesus. Like Jesus, the Lamb of God who was led to the slaughter without resistance, Stephen knelt in an attitude of prayer and worship as angry men began hurling stones at him. Stephen was humble and faithful to the message of the gospel in word and deed, and God was honored. So much so that Stephen's vision of Jesus is of Him standing rather than sitting. Stephen died with a vision of His exalted Lord in his mind and immediately stepped into His presence. In the end, Stephen not only testified about the centrality of the gospel, he also lived that truth.

CHRIST CONNECTION

In his death as the first Christian martyr, Stephen followed in the footsteps of His Savior. Both Jesus and Stephen were falsely accused and charged for blasphemy. Both Jesus and Stephen prayed for their executioners. Both Jesus and Stephen entrusted their spirits to God as they died. As a follower of Jesus Christ, Stephen reflected his Master in life and in death and will again at the resurrection.

OUR MISSION

Head

How have you seen Christians be falsely accused?

What role does the Holy Spirit play in our response to opposition?

Heart

Why do you think people respond better to a humble person than an arrogant one?

What are some ways our inner motives of love can be outwardly demonstrated?

Hands

How have you seen faithful suffering encourage believers?

How have you seen suffering open doors to sharing the gospel with unbelievers?

PERSONAL STUDY: DAY 1

⭐ **The point: The disciples focused on preaching and appointed others to care for the physical needs of the church.**

▶ Read Acts 6:1-7.

What was the complaint from the Hellenistic Jews and what caused their issue?

The Twelve appointed _____ individuals to care for the widows. They did this in order to continue focusing on other aspects of ministry. What aspects did the Twelve remain focused on? What was the result of this act of sharing ministry?

Consider the qualifications the disciples were looking for in the men to take on the duties of caring for the physical needs of the church members. Why would it be important to have such high standards?

▶ Respond

Think of a time when you felt overwhelmed, like you had too much on your plate. Then, ask God to help you see how to focus on your specific role in building up the church.

Do you currently serve in a specific role in your church? If you do not currently have a regular duty at your church, think about what you are good at and how you can use that to serve. Check the church website, weekly calendar, or just ask around to find ways you can help out.

⭐ **The point: Stephen remained faithful to Jesus even when falsely accused.**

Think about a recent argument you had or overheard. Who was on the side of truth? What are the advantages to being on the side of truth? Explain.

▶ **Read Acts 6:8-15.**

How do you think being on truth's side and being filled with the Holy Spirit gave Stephen the confidence to boldly teach truth to hostile people?

When have you experienced something similar? What happened?

How can you have the same confidence as Stephen for similar situations in the future?

▶ **Respond**

Defending your faith can feel intimidating—to defend what you believe, you have to understand what you believe. Commit to finding a mentor who will spend time in the Bible with you and help you grow in your faith.

For further study on defending your faith, read *Big Questions: Developing a Christ-Centered Apologetic* by Andy McLean.

PERSONAL STUDY: DAY 3

⭐ **The point: Stephen referenced the twelve patriarchs to testify about Jesus.**

▶ Read Acts 7:1-16.

Stephen pointed to the reality of Israel as God's people, but he also pointed to the necessity of faith. How did faith play into the building of God's people? *(Hint: Think of Abraham and Isaac, Joseph, Moses and Pharaoh, Rahab, Ruth, David and Saul, etc.)*

Why do you think Stephen referred to Israel's history in order to share the gospel? How do you think this would have affected the Jewish leaders?

In this passage, how do you see the importance of looking to the past in order to understand the truth of present events?

Why is it important to realize that God's promises to us often include suffering along with blessing?

▶ Respond

Think of a past experience in your life that was tough at the time, but through which God blessed you as a result. What did you learn from that experience? How can this help you in future difficulties?

It is possible to encourage others with your story (2 Cor. 1:4). Share what you have learned about faithfulness and God's blessings with a friend who is currently in a tough situation.

PERSONAL STUDY: DAY 4

⭐ **The point: Stephen pointed back to Moses to testify about Jesus.**

▶ Review Exodus 2:14; 3:5-8,10,17. Focus on three things as you read:

- The Israelites questioned Moses as their leader.
- When God revealed Himself to Moses, He introduced Himself as the God of Moses' ancestors.
- God's response when His people are oppressed is not to sit by and do nothing, even when it seems that He is silent.

▶ Read Acts 7:17-36.

The Jews considered Moses and the Law extremely significant. Describe how Stephen's speech might have connected with them.

How do you think Stephen's message might have offended the religious leaders? How do you think it might have comforted the oppressed believers?

What connections did Stephen make between Moses and Jesus?

▶ Respond

What is a story in the Bible that encourages you? Summarize the story and explain how it encourages you in your faith.

Both Jesus and Moses were rejected leaders. Sometimes people will reject you for taking a stand for truth. When have you experienced this personally? How can you prepare now to respond similarly to Stephen in those situations?

PERSONAL STUDY: DAY 5

⭐ The point: Stephen discussed Israel's rebellion.

Have you ever considered yourself a rebel? Sometimes, rebellion can be a good thing. For example, we often have to rebel against things our friends try to talk us into or the activities our culture tells us are normal, even though God's Word says otherwise. However, when God's people rebel against Him, it is never a good thing.

▶ Read Acts 7:37-43.

Compare the Israelites' rebellion against God in asking Aaron to make gods for them and the religious leaders' rebellion against Jesus.

Making gods	Rejecting Jesus

What are some ways you see people rejecting Jesus or rebelling against God today? What are some of the "gods" they worship?

Like Stephen, how can we help the people around us see God's truth?

▶ Respond

Think about your own life. How are you tempted to rebel against God?

Ask God to help you stand strong in the face of temptation, to rebel against evil rather than rebelling against Him. Pray that He would work through you so that others would see His love and truth in your life.

THE GOSPEL EXPANDS

*GOD CALLS US TO BE FAITHFUL
AND OBEDIENT WITNESSES.*

INTRODUCTION

Connection. Coincidence. Happy accident. By chance. Luck of the draw. All of these words or phrases describe an unexpected meeting of people or details that would otherwise be completely unconnected. For example, a guy finding a telephone number on a slip of paper in the middle of a theme park with the name "Ben" written on it; then calling the number and finding on the other end of the line his best friend from elementary school.

 When have you experienced a coincidence? What happened?

While these occurrences may seem random, believers know God is sovereign over all things. As in today's session, Philip taking a different road was not a coincidence, but part of God's plan. In the same way, we can view coincidences in our own lives as opportunities from God.

SETTING THE CONTEXT

The martyrdom of Stephen marked a significant escalation in the attacks against the early Christians and their gospel message. So severe was the persecution that all the Christians except the apostles scattered. Significantly, it's during this period of persecution that we are introduced to Saul, who approved of the killing of Stephen and emerged as the chief persecutor of the church.

Philip was one of the men appointed to take care of the needs of the church members. When the persecution began, Philip traveled to Samaria. The map on "Expansion of the Early Church in Palestine" (p. 34) traces the route Philip took after spreading out from the persecution in Jerusalem. Going to the Samaritans crossed a significant cultural line. Jews considered Samaritans as members of a lower class and as half-breeds because they descended from Jews who had intermarried with Gentiles.

Despite the cultural barriers, Philip proclaimed the gospel message to the Samaritans. God also used Philip to perform miracles in Samaria, which confirmed the truth of his message. Philip is the first missionary in the Book of Acts, but he would not be the last; he would be the first among many.

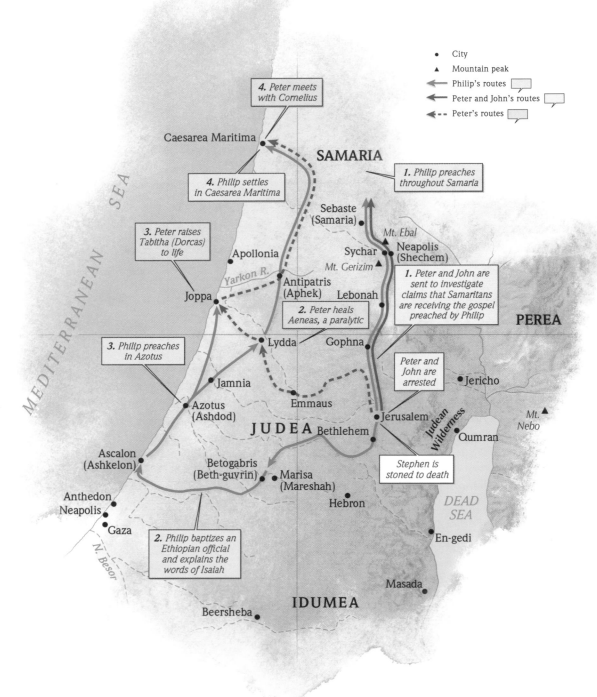

EXPANSION OF THE
EARLY CHURCH IN PALESTINE

Legend:
- • City
- ▲ Mountain peak
- ← Philip's routes
- ← Peter and John's routes
- ◄--- Peter's routes

4. Peter meets with Cornelius

4. Philip settles in Caesarea Maritima

3. Peter raises Tabitha (Dorcas) to life

1. Philip preaches throughout Samaria

1. Peter and John are sent to investigate claims that Samaritans are receiving the gospel preached by Philip

2. Peter heals Aeneas, a paralytic

Peter and John are arrested

3. Philip preaches in Azotus

Stephen is stoned to death

2. Philip baptizes an Ethiopian official and explains the words of Isaiah

Places:
SAMARIA
Caesarea Maritima
Sebaste (Samaria)
Mt. Ebal
Neapolis (Shechem)
Sychar
Mt. Gerizim
Apollonia
Yarkon R.
Antipatris (Aphek)
Lebonah
PEREA
Joppa
Lydda
Gophna
Jericho
Jamnia
Emmaus
Mt. Nebo
Azotus (Ashdod)
Jerusalem
Judean Wilderness
Qumran
JUDEA
Bethlehem
Ascalon (Ashkelon)
Betogabris (Beth-guvrin)
Marisa (Mareshah)
DEAD SEA
Anthedon
Neapolis
Hebron
En-gedi
Gaza
N. Besor
Masada
IDUMEA
Beersheba
MEDITERRANEAN SEA

SESSION VIDEOS

Watch this session's video, and then continue the group discussion using the following guide.

▶ What ideas or phrases stood out to you most in the video? Why?

▶ How, specifically, does this story encourage you in sharing your faith?

GROUP DISCUSSION

As a group, read Acts 8:26-29.

★ How would you describe Philip's response to the Spirit's instructions? What does this tell us about Philip?

▶ How is Philip's situation similar to one you could experience?

This story is significant in the Book of Acts. For starters, during that time, Ethiopia was about as far away as you could get. Talking about Ethiopia would be like talking about the other side of the world, even though these regions don't seem so far apart on modern maps. In the minds of the original readers of Acts, the introduction of an Ethiopian to the story was a big deal. Especially one who had to come to Jerusalem in search of God. This story introduces the global scope of the gospel message—it's a word for the nations, not just the Jews.

Philip was sent by God to be on mission for Him. Upon hearing the angel's command, Philip obeyed immediately. Just a few verses earlier, Philip was enjoying a thriving ministry in Samaria (8:4-8). One could imagine that a command like this—to undertake a lengthy journey, prompted only by the voice of God—might be met with some inner resistance. Any thriving work is difficult to leave and doing so takes a great deal of faith.

▶ Philip's response was immediate. If you had a thriving ministry like Philip and God asked you to leave, how would you respond?

▶ When has God asked you to leave something familiar for the unknown?

GROUP DISCUSSION *CONT.*

As a group, read Acts 8:30-35.

▶ What might have happened had Philip been unprepared to talk about Scripture or been unfamiliar with Isaiah's prophecy?

▶ What does this tell us about the connection between personal spiritual growth and spreading the good news of Jesus?

★ What can we learn from Philip's approach to sharing the gospel?

Philip didn't have the credentials of a Bible scholar or a teacher of the law—he was an ordinary guy. However, because he was filled with the Spirit and because of what he'd seen and experienced in his own life of faith, he responded with confidence and clarity. They read a passage from Isaiah, and the Ethiopian invited Philip to explain it. This gave Philip a starting point to share the gospel with the man.

The whole story of the Bible, from one end to the other, points to Jesus. The story of Israel and the whole of the Old Testament are about anticipating Jesus. We see it in how they longed for a king, though all their kings fell short of the glory they aspired to. We see it in the high demands of the law, which nobody can attain. We see it in the countless sorrows described in the Psalms and Prophets, where the brokenness of the world was displayed and the people cried out, "How long, O Lord?" Jesus embodies all that the Old Testament longs for and points to. Even the broader story of the Old Testament—exile from the garden of Eden, longing for the promised land, and exile (again) at the hands of the Babylonians—points to Jesus as the conquering King who defeats Satan, sin, and death and brings us back to God.

▶ Like Philip, you probably aren't a Bible scholar. What are some ways you can use Scripture you know to share the gospel and point others to Jesus, right where you are?

As a group, read Acts 8:36-40.

⭐ What did the man's question in verse 36 reveal? How does this reflect a changed heart?

▶ What does verse 40 teach us about Philip's continued faithfulness?

Philip's words were good news for the man because he believed the message of the gospel. His heart was changed, and Philip was obedient to Jesus' command to baptize those who come to faith. Then Philip was taken away miraculously— not taken by the Spirit away from ministry but toward new ministry. God had another appointment for Philip to share the gospel elsewhere.

CHRIST CONNECTION

The Ethiopian eunuch was familiar with the Old Testament prophets but was unable to understand how their message was fulfilled in Jesus Christ. Philip was led by the Holy Spirit to help the eunuch understand how Jesus died on the cross for our sins and was raised from the dead, in accordance with the ancient prophecies.

OUR MISSION

 Head

Do you think it is possible to tell the good news about Jesus from anywhere in the Scriptures? Why or why not?

What are some ways you've been surprised by how God has led you, your church, or your friends to be on mission?

V Heart

What are some reasons we might feel intimidated to try explaining the Scriptures to an unbeliever?

How can we cultivate hearts willing to respond obediently to the Spirit's leading, no matter the risks?

Hands

What are some ways you can do the work of a Spirit-empowered evangelist in the coming days?

Where are some places in your life where you imagine this work will take place?

PERSONAL STUDY: DAY 1

⭐ ## The point: Saul persecuted the church.

Look back at Acts 7. What was the breaking point? What caused the Christians to disperse? Who stayed behind?

▶ ### Read Acts 8:1-3.

Saul was one of the major persecutors of the early church. In what ways did he persecute the church?

What caused Saul to act violently against the Christians?

What do you think motivates people to persecute others today? Explain.

▶ ### Respond

Americans enjoy a relative freedom of religious practices, but believers in countries that are hostile to the faith experience beatings, social shunning, imprisonment, and sometimes death.

If you knew that persecution was a possibility for you, how would you prepare mentally, spiritually, emotionally, and physically?

For further study on persecution, read Jeremiah 20:11; Matthew 5:10-12; John 15:18-20; and 1 Peter 4:12-14,16.

⭐ **The point: Philip ministered in Samaria.**

▶ Read Acts 8:4-8.

Though the threat of persecution increased the believers' fear, there were some positive results; it forced the early Christians out of Jerusalem to surrounding towns.

Where did Philip travel when all the believers dispersed? Where else is this place mentioned in the Bible?

Describe what kind of message Philip shared where he traveled.

What was the general attitude about Philip's ministry there? Why do you think this was so different from the place Philip fled?

List the three ways the crowds interacted with Philip.

What happened as Philip ministered in their city?

How do people typically respond to the gospel message today?

▶ Respond

One of the major challenges of being a believer is that we have to step outside our comfort zones, talk to people different from us, and share Jesus with them.

List the names of a few people who need to hear the gospel. Then, in your journal, jot down some ideas of ways you can share with them.

For further study on reaching out to those different from us, read Jonah 1–4; Luke 10:25-37; and Acts 10.

PERSONAL STUDY: DAY 3

⭐ **The point: Philip obeyed the Lord on the desert road.**

On a scale of 1-10, rank how likely you are to do the following:

___ When my mom asks me to clean my room, I immediately get to work.

___ I complete my homework and turn it in by the due date.

___ When my coach tells us to run ten laps, I do so without complaining.

God calls us to obey Him and to obey our authority figures, unless they tell us to do something that goes against His Word.

▶ **Read Acts 8:26-29.**

Highlight the phrase "so he got up and went" (v. 27). What had to happen before Philip would obey?

How is Philip's obedience a good example to us?

▶ **Respond**

Philip had a thriving ministry in Samaria, but when God asked him to leave, Philip didn't hesitate. When has God called you from a comfortable situation into something unknown?

PERSONAL STUDY: DAY 4

⭐ **The point: Philip guided the Ethiopian official through the Scriptures.**

▶ **Read Acts 8:30-35.**

Philip may not have been a biblical scholar, but he was ready to share the gospel when he had the opportunity.

How did Philip use the passage in Isaiah as a starting point to tell this man about Jesus?

What does this passage teach about the value of knowing God's Word, especially when it comes to sharing your faith?

▶ **Respond**

Draw a circle in the middle of a blank page. Write Sharing the Gospel in the center of the circle. Create a bubble map as you think of different Scriptures you can use to share the gospel.

For further study on sharing the gospel with others, read *Sharing the Gospel without Freaking Out* by Alvin L. Reid (B&H Academic, 2017).

PERSONAL STUDY: DAY 5

⭐ **The point: Philip led the official to profess his faith in Christ and be baptized.**

▶ Read Acts 8:36-40.

The Ethiopian's question might seem simple to us today, but religious leaders in that day likely would have said: He's not an ethnic Jew. He's a foreigner. Why should we baptize him? But the Ethiopian asked the opposite: What reason was there for him not to be baptized?

Briefly explain what happened in Philip's earlier conversation with the Ethiopian. How did this prepare the man to be baptized?

What surprises you about the Ethiopian's request? What surprises you about Philip's response? Explain.

Why do you think it is sometimes difficult to obey God when He calls us to people who are different from us?

▶ Respond

Think about a time when God obviously provided an opportunity for you to share the gospel. How can these situations encourage you to share the gospel in the future? .

It's easy sometimes to just stick to the facts when sharing the gospel. List two ways you can invite people to join you in following Jesus.

SAUL IS SAVED

ONLY JESUS CAN TRANSFORM HEARTS AND TURN LIVES AROUND FOR HIS GLORY.

INTRODUCTION

Before becoming the superhero we know, Wonder Woman was an Amazon princess named Diana. The population of her entire island was made up of female warriors. The island was all the world she knew until a pilot crashed there. He told her about the war consuming the world (World War I), and she decided to use her superpowers to help them. On her island, her strength may have been normal, though greater than some. But when she stepped out into the world, her strength transformed into a superpower.

▶ What other superheroes can you think of who have different identities or transform into something else to fight crime?

Transformations like these are obvious. The differences between Wonder Woman and the rest of humanity were obvious. In a similar way, Paul was the best of the best when it came to the Pharisees. As a Christian, the difference was obvious—he was completely transformed.

SETTING THE CONTEXT

The Bible first introduces us to Saul at the stoning of Stephen. Saul was at least a cheering bystander, if not an active participant, during the first Christian martyrdom. Saul was a Roman citizen, born in Tarsus of Cilicia. But according to his own testimony, he was brought up in an idealistically Jewish fashion. His parents were Pharisees, strict adherents to the law. Being brought up in this environment, Saul was staunchly religious, holding himself and others to the highest legal standard. As a strict Jew, Saul refused to associate with anything unclean, especially Gentiles.

As a Pharisee, Saul saw Christianity as blasphemy. The idea that God could become a man was, in his mind, an affront to the holiness of Yahweh. So severe was this offense that Saul believed it should be punishable by death, as it was with Stephen, so he made it his life's mission to root out other Christians. But God had a different future in mind for Saul, which would involve him going by his Greek name. "Paul's Life" (p. 46) provides an overview of that future.

PAUL'S *LIFE*

THE PHARISEE	• A Jew born in Tarsus but trained in Jerusalem by Gamaliel; zealous for God (Acts 22:3) • Supported the stoning of Stephen and persecuted the church; traveled to Damascus to arrest believers and bring them back to Jerusalem (7:58; 8:1,3; 9:1-2; 22:4-5)
THE CHRISTIAN	• Met Jesus on the way to Damascus and was blinded; three days later, he was healed by Ananias so he could see, filled with the Holy Spirit, and baptized (9:3-18) • Proclaimed Jesus in the synagogues in Damascus and later in Jerusalem (9:20-30) • Found by Barnabas in Tarsus; taken to Antioch to help teach the disciples (11:25-26)
THE MISSIONARY	• Saul and Barnabas set apart by the Spirit for missionary calling (13:1-3) • *First Missionary Journey* (13:4–14:28) • Saul sent with Barnabas to the Jerusalem Council, which discussed and affirmed salvation by faith for Gentiles (15:1-35) • *Second Missionary Journey* (15:36–18:22) • *Third Missionary Journey* (18:23–21:19) • Arrested in Jerusalem; defended his faith before kings and rulers; appealed to Caesar and sent to Rome, where he proclaimed Jesus while under house arrest (21:26–28:31) • According to tradition, released from house arrest but then arrested a second time and imprisoned in Rome, and later beheaded

SESSION VIDEOS

Watch this session's video, and then continue the group discussion using the following guide.

▶ What ideas or phrases stood out to you most in the video? Why?

▶ What is your biggest takeaway when you think about the conversion of Saul?

GROUP DISCUSSION

As a group, read Acts 9:3-9.

⭐ What do you think Jesus wanted to teach Saul through his blindness?

▶ Given his background, what might Saul have been thinking about during those three days of blindness and fasting?

Saul approached Damascus, planning on capturing and eliminating those who followed Jesus of Nazareth. On his way, he encountered a voice, an overwhelmingly bright light, and a question. The question confused Saul. He did not recognize the voice as Jesus because he did not know Jesus. Jesus identified Himself as the One being persecuted, because Saul was persecuting His followers. What Saul was doing to the disciples, he was actually doing to Christ Himself. At that moment, humiliation and humility began to set in. The world as Saul knew it was about to change.

Jesus instructed Saul to go into the city and wait for instructions. Saul's traveling companions were stunned by what they could hear but not see. However, they weren't the only ones who couldn't see. Saul had become blind. The author, Luke, described Saul like this: "though his eyes were open, he could see nothing" (v. 8). This was a clear reference back to Jesus' teachings when He had called the Jewish religious leaders "blind guides" multiple times in Matthew 23. The men led Saul by the hand to Damascus. He did not arrive as a protector of the Jewish faith as he had intended, but as a blind, humbled man waiting to hear from the very One he had come to persecute. Broken for the first time in his life, Saul did not see, eat, or drink for three days.

▶ In what ways do you think Saul's thoughts about Jesus started to change in that moment? What about the way he thought about himself?

GROUP DISCUSSION *CONT.*

As a group, read Acts 9:10-16.

▶ How do you think Ananias felt when the Lord instructed him to take care of Saul?

★ What does God's plan for Saul reveal about His power and purposes?

Ananias's response of "Here I am, Lord" revealed a heart that was eager to please the Lord and obey Him. Where most Christians would have looked at Saul with warranted fear and trepidation, God wanted Ananias to see a "chosen instrument" He would use to carry the gospel to the known world. We must not write off anyone, even those who are hostile to the faith, because God's power in the gospel can melt even the hardest heart.

As a group, read Acts 9:17-20.

★ What is significant about the way Ananias addressed Saul?

▶ What does Ananias' response to God's direction reveal about his faith?

▶ What stands out to you about what Saul did shortly after being baptized?

God could have healed Saul without the personal interaction with another believer, but God has never intended anyone to live for Him apart from the fellowship of the church. When Ananias addressed Saul as brother, he was affirming Saul's new relationship with the church. He was no longer a persecutor of the faith; he was now part of the family of faith. After Saul was baptized, he began proclaiming the One he had scorned. Though Saul did not know everything about following Christ, he knew enough to begin sharing the gospel with those around him.

Most of the early church probably saw Saul in only one way: an enemy of the gospel to be avoided at all cost. But God taught them, and us, a vital lesson through the conversion of Saul. No one is outside of the scope of God's generous grace. No one is beyond the reach of Jesus Christ. God's power to save has no limit and could even extend to one of the world's most militant persecutors of Jesus Christ—Saul of Tarsus. If the gospel could transform Saul, it can transform anyone.

The God who delights in doing the unexpected didn't stop with Saul's conversion. God transformed Saul through the power of the gospel and graciously called him to be the greatest missionary in history. God's conversion and calling of Saul reveals His heart as the God who sends.

▶ When have you been tempted to view someone as too far beyond the reach of God's redemptive power? Why? How might the story of Saul's conversion change your perspective?

CHRIST CONNECTION

The conversion and calling of Saul is a demonstration of God's power to save. Through an encounter with the crucified and risen Jesus, this once-hardened persecutor of God's people began his journey to become the greatest missionary the world has ever known. Only the gospel can transform a public opponent of Christ into a fervent witness to His salvation.

OUR MISSION

 Head

What are some of the challenges we often face when it comes to sharing the gospel with others?

How does Saul's story of conversion deepen your own gratitude for God's grace and mercy?

Heart

God used a unique collision with Saul to get his attention. In what ways do you see Jesus "colliding" with people today?

What is at the heart of your story of following Jesus? How can you tell your story in a compelling way?

Hands

We normally think of being sent by God as being sent to share the gospel to unbelievers. How does God send us to other believers too?

Ananias needed courage to obey Jesus and go to Saul. How can we have courage to obey God no matter what?

PERSONAL STUDY: DAY 1

⭐ **The point: Saul was called out of persecution.**

Before you dig into today's study, read Acts 8:1-3 and summarize what happened and what Saul's (Paul's Hebrew name) role was in all that took place.

▶ Read Acts 9:1-2.

Saul was introduced in Acts 8 because of his involvement with Stephen's murder. Even after this, Saul continued persecuting Christians.

What did Saul request from the high priest?

At this point, what kind of person would you say Saul was?

Why do you think Saul persecuted Christians? Why do people sometimes persecute Christians today?

Saul, as a member of the Sanhedrin, most likely thought he was doing a good thing by persecuting these people who he thought distorted the message of true Judaism.

▶ Respond

Ask yourself: If I was a Christian living in Saul's day, how would I feel if I heard about Saul persecuting Christians?

Jot down the name of someone you're afraid to share the gospel with. Then, ask God to give you the courage to do so.

Christians today are still persecuted. How can you pray for those who suffer because of their faith in Jesus?

⭐ **The point: Saul's trip to Damascus was not what he intended.**

▶ Read Acts 9:3-9.

What instructions did Jesus give to Saul?

Saul had been _____ blind before this encounter, then he became

_____ blind.

Compare and contrast Saul's life before and after encountering Jesus.

Before Jesus	After Jesus

Does Saul appear to be receptive to the message of his encounter with Jesus? Why or why not?

▶ Respond

Imagine how it would have felt to encounter Jesus in the dramatic way that Saul did. How would you have felt if this was your first real encounter with Jesus?

Fill in the following: Saul's plans changed from persecuting _____ to making

_____. God has changed my plans of _____ to _____.

For further study on Saul's life before Christ, read Acts 26:1-11 and Philippians 3:3-6.

PERSONAL STUDY: DAY 3

⭐ **The point: God called Ananias to go to Saul.**

▶ Read Acts 9:10-16.

God revealed the next step in His plan to a disciple named Ananias.

There are two visions mentioned in this passage. Describe each vision.

First	Second

How did Ananias respond when he heard the Lord speaking in the vision?

What was Saul doing when he received the vision from the Lord? Why was this activity important?

If Saul's life had not been changed on the road to Damascus, what could have happened to Ananias?

▶ Respond

God calls all believers to obey certain tasks (ex. share the gospel) and calls some people to specific tasks (ex. share the gospel with a specific unreached people group).

For further study on God's call, read Jeremiah 1:5; Luke 9:1-6; and 2 Timothy 1:8-12.

PERSONAL STUDY: DAY 4

⭐ **The point: God restored Saul's sight and he was baptized.**

▶ Read Acts 9:17-18.

Why is it significant that Ananias called Saul "brother"?

Draw or describe what you think this scene must have looked like.

List the two reasons Ananias said the Lord had sent him to Saul (v. 17c)?

How did Ananias' actions confirm what God had done through all of Saul's experiences on this trip? How do you think that confirmation helped Saul begin his new faith?

Saul's baptism was a symbol of the change that God had now brought about in his life. How had Saul's life already changed?

▶ Respond

Salvation changes us from being God's enemies to being His family.

Have you been baptized after deciding to follow Jesus? If not, take a next step this week by talking to someone in your church about professing your faith through baptism.

For further study on baptism, read Matthew 28:19-20; Acts 10:44-48; and Romans 6:4.

PERSONAL STUDY: DAY 5

⭐ ## The point: Saul began preaching about Jesus as the Messiah.

When has something changed your life so radically that you immediately began talking about it with everyone you knew?

▶ ## Read Acts 9:20-25.

Saul didn't waste any time once he regained his sight. What did he "immediately" do after being baptized?

Why were the Jews confused when they heard Saul's preaching? How did they respond to him (v. 23)?

This chapter is a major turning point in both Saul's life and the life of the new church. How had the situation changed completely from the beginning of Acts 9 to this point in today's passage?

Saul's disciples helped him escape persecution (v. 25). What does the fact that Saul so quickly made disciples tell you about the effectiveness of his ministry in Damascus?

▶ ## Respond

When was the last time you explained the gospel clearly to someone who needed to hear it? How did they respond?

On a blank piece of paper, list the core elements needed to share the gospel with someone. Then, list the names of people you need to share the gospel with currently.

THE MISSION
IS EMBRACED

*GOD CALLS HIS CHURCH TO SEND AND SUPPORT
MISSIONARIES TO THOSE WHO HAVE NEVER
HEARD THE GOSPEL.*

INTRODUCTION

Have you ever been on a mission trip? Maybe you worked on houses—painting, building wheelchair ramps, or landscaping. Maybe you led a Vacation Bible School in a small town, inner-city area, or foreign country. Maybe you packed and delivered boxed lunches or did face-painting at a church function.

▶ Where have you gone on mission trips and what did you do?

We see God's method of sending missionaries all throughout the Book of Acts, and if we pay attention to the big story of Scripture, we see this plan throughout the Bible. God is a sending God. Page after page of Scripture shows how God sent His people out to make Him known, but we can see this most clearly in the incarnation.

Jesus was sent. God Himself left His place of glory, took on the flesh, and dwelt among people to reveal God's goodness and His plan to redeem them. Sending and going is the very heart of God, and it should be for us as well.

SETTING THE CONTEXT

God was clear that the gospel was not a message for the Jews alone. As the Book of Acts continues, the church grows in her understanding of this key truth. Peter, for example, was given a vision from God that was followed by a divine appointment with a Gentile named Cornelius. Peter came to understand that he should proclaim the good news of the gospel to anyone who would hear.

Meanwhile, the gospel was spread by those who had been scattered after Stephen's martyrdom. The church in Antioch became the first multiethnic congregation and would soon give birth to the first great missionary-sending movement of the church, represented by "The First Missionary Journey of Paul" (p. 58).

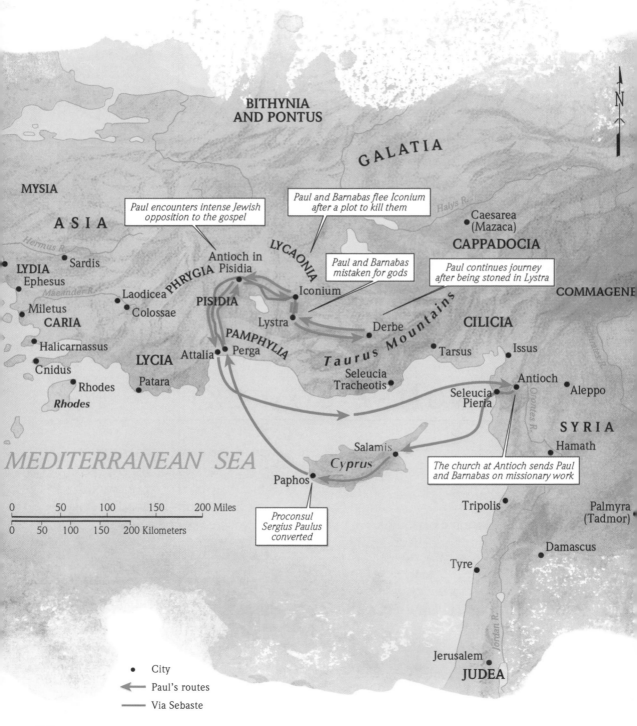

THE FIRST
MISSIONARY JOURNEY OF PAUL

BITHYNIA AND PONTUS

GALATIA

N

MYSIA

Halys R.

Caesarea
(Mazaca)

CAPPADOCIA

ASIA

Hermus R.

LYCAONIA

Paul and Barnabas flee Iconium
after a plot to kill them

LYDIA • Sardis

Ephesus •

Antioch in
Pisidia

Paul encounters intense Jewish
opposition to the gospel

Paul and Barnabas
mistaken for gods

Paul continues journey
after being stoned in Lystra

COMMAGENE

Maeander R.

Laodicea •

PHRYGIA

Iconium •

Miletus •

Colossae •

PISIDIA

CARIA

Lystra •

Derbe •

CILICIA

Halicarnassus •

PAMPHYLIA

Taurus Mountains

Cnidus •

LYCIA

Attalia • Perga

• Tarsus

Issus •

Rhodes •

Patara •

Seleucia
Tracheotis •

Antioch •

• Aleppo

Rhodes

Seleucia
Pieria

SYRIA

Orontes R.

MEDITERRANEAN SEA

Salamis

• Hamath

Cyprus

Paphos •

The church at Antioch sends Paul
and Barnabas on missionary work

0   50   100   150   200 Miles

Tripolis •

Palmyra
(Tadmor)

0   50   100   150   200 Kilometers

Proconsul
Sergius Paulus
converted

Damascus •

Tyre •

Jordan R.

Jerusalem •

JUDEA

• City

⟵ Paul's routes

—— Via Sebaste

SESSION VIDEOS

Watch this session's video, and then continue the group discussion using the following guide.

▶ What ideas or phrases stood out to you most in the video? Why?

▶ What is the role of the Holy Spirit in the church and in missionaries?

GROUP DISCUSSION

As a group, read Acts 13:1-3.

★ How would you describe the priorities of the church at Antioch based on these verses?

▶ What were some of the reasons the church could have given for not sending out Paul and Barnabas?

▶ Why do you think it was important for the missionaries to have a church as a sending base?

As the leaders were worshiping and fasting, they heard from the Holy Spirit. These leaders, and the church, were in the right posture to hear from God and respond accordingly when the time came.

The Holy Spirit instructed them to set apart Barnabas and Paul for the work God had called them to do. God separated these two men from the normal rhythms of being part of the church at Antioch for something else. Barnabas and Paul would leave their church and life as they knew it in Antioch to advance the gospel to unreached regions as missionaries.

▶ When have you experienced a church praying over or sending off people to do short- or long-term mission work? How does that experience compare to what happened to Barnabas and Paul?

GROUP DISCUSSION *CONT.*

As a group, read Acts 13:4-8.

⭐ How would you describe the missionaries' ministry philosophy based on these verses?

▶ Is it right to expect opposition when we proclaim the gospel? Why or why not?

So Paul and Barnabas headed across the island declaring the message to any who would listen, until they ran across a false prophet. This man served as an attendant of the Roman proconsul who wanted to hear the word of God. But Elymas the sorcerer did not want that to happen; he wanted to turn the proconsul away from the gospel message. We should not be surprised.

Just because God guides us to share the gospel, we should not expect the road in doing so to be without opposition. That's because the gospel, by its very nature, is divisive. Think for a moment about what people must accept when they hear the message of Jesus.

They must accept the news about themselves that they are sinners, dead in their own sin. They must accept that they cannot do anything to change this condition and instead are at the mercy of God. Then they must accept that Jesus loves them enough to die in their place, though they do not deserve it. And they must accept that Jesus rose from the dead, nonsense to the world. These are difficult truths, but they are an all-or-nothing proposition.

This brings us back to the core of what we believe. Perhaps our failure to share the gospel is, many times, less about our preparation and more an indictment on our own confidence in the power of the message we are to proclaim. Do we really believe the truth of the gospel? If we do, then we will be witnesses to the power of God through that message.

As a group, read Acts 13:9-12.

⭐ What purpose did the miracle of judgment serve in this passage?

How is this consistent with the purpose of miracles in the ministry of Jesus?

Paul and Barnabas understood that their primary mission was centered on the gospel message. They were, first and foremost, to be witnesses to the life, death, and resurrection of Christ. If that was their goal, then everything else must contribute to that goal. In other words, there were no isolated miracles, no random signs. Rather, the miraculous good that happened through these missionaries served the greater purpose of validating the message.

CHRIST CONNECTION

Jesus told His disciples that the gates of hell would not prevail against His church, reminding us that God's people are "on offense," continuing the mission Jesus began. God's plan is for Christians to take the powerful and good news of Jesus to places of deep spiritual darkness with full confidence that Jesus will build His church.

OUR MISSION

Head

How do you see yourself—through what you do or who God has made you to be in Christ?

Why does it matter how we see ourselves? How does your understanding of your identity frame how you live each day?

Heart

How does experiencing hardship and suffering advance the gospel?

What are some ways you were encouraged by someone else and then able to act in faith?

Hands

How are you making disciples of Jesus wherever you are?

How do you support missionaries sent by your local church?

PERSONAL STUDY: DAY 1

⭐ **The point: God sends out missionaries through His church.**

▶ Read Acts 13:1-3.

Highlight the two characteristics of the people mentioned in verse 1.

What two things were the members of the Antioch church doing when the Spirit spoke?

The church at Antioch was prepared. They were living in such a way that they recognized the Spirit when He spoke and were able to respond to what He said.

Name the two men who were set apart.

In your own words, describe the task God gave these men.

Have you seen anything similar to this in your own church? Explain.

▶ Respond

On an index card, list the names of missionaries or people you know who are preparing to go on a mission trip. Keep this index card with you throughout the week and pray for the people listed each time you see the card.

We are all called to share the gospel. Whether in your own home or across the world, you should strive to reach out with the message of hope that you have. What is your greatest obstacle to sharing your faith? Who do you know that needs to hear the gospel? How can you share the gospel with them when you have the opportunity?

PERSONAL STUDY: DAY 2

⭐ **The point: Paul and Barnabas journeyed to Cyprus where they encountered a sorcerer.**

▶ Read Acts 13:4-12.

Where were Paul and Barnabas when this took place? Who sent them there?

Who did the men encounter in this passage and what were their titles?

What happened in order for Paul and Barnabas to meet Elymas?

List the charges against the false prophet and the punishment that was given.

Charge	Punishment

Do you think this punishment was too harsh? Too lenient? Why or why not?

▶ Respond

God sent the men to Cyprus, the home of Barnabas. How do you think God prepares those He intends to send today?

What questions do you have after reading this passage today? What would your response have been if you had witnessed this account? Write your thoughts and questions below and seek out a friend to think it through together.

PERSONAL STUDY: DAY 3

⭐ **The point: Paul taught in Antioch.**

▶ Read Acts 13:13-41.

What three important facts set the stage for the mission?

Paul and Barnabas were in _____ _____.

They went to the _____ on the _____.

This passage includes Paul's first sermon. What was he reminding his fellow Jewish people of as he recounted their history?

Essentially, Paul spoke about the truth of the gospel, the history of the gospel, and how Jesus came to fulfill God's promise.

What did Paul say was being proclaimed to these people (vv. 38-39)?

How do people often miss the point when it comes to the gospel?

▶ Respond

Imagine that you're hearing Paul's sermon in person—how do you respond? How do your friends and family respond? What would your next steps be after hearing what Paul had to say?

The point of Paul's message was to point people toward Jesus. Do you have people in your circle of influence who have missed the point? List their names and commit to praying every day this week that God would give you an opportunity to share Jesus with them.

PERSONAL STUDY: DAY 4

⭐ **The point: Paul and Barnabas were driven out of Antioch.**

▶ Read Acts 13:42-52.

Even after Paul's warning about not truly understanding what they heard, the people initially wanted to hear more about Jesus. They even asked Paul and Barnabas to return the next week to continue teaching.

What happened when Paul and Barnabas returned to teach?

Highlight the ways the Jews responded when they saw the crowds.

Summarize how Paul and Barnabas responded to the opposition from the Jews.

The Gentiles and Jews had a completely different responses to the news that Paul and Barnabas would be taking the gospel to the Gentiles from then on. Describe how each responded.

Jews	Gentiles

Why were Paul and Barnabas driven out of Antioch? How did they respond to that?

▶ Respond

While the Jews hungered for God's Word, they ultimately allowed jealousy to win and forced the missionaries and their message out of the city. Have you ever been rejected or experienced people pushing you away because you have tried to share Jesus with them or do the right thing?

On a note card or the notes app on your phone, record the ways you can be encouraged by the way Paul and Barnabas responded to opposition in this passage. Keep this with you as a reminder.

PERSONAL STUDY: DAY 5

⭐ **The point: Many believed in Jesus in Iconium, but Paul and Barnabas fled due to persecution.**

▶ Read Acts 14:1-7.

When Paul began to preach in the synagogue in Iconium, who believed? Why is this important?

What happened in verse 2? What kind of pattern is this?

Despite the circumstances, they continued to boldly share the gospel.

Underline in your Bible what God performed through them (v. 3).

How did the unbelieving Jews and Gentiles treat Paul and Barnabas?

Ultimately, what did the missionaries decide to do?

How do their actions provide an example for the way we should handle persecution today?

▶ Respond

It's difficult to imagine what Paul and Barnabas must have experienced when people rejected their message and wanted to stone them. Though they faced persecution, they remained faithful to God and the mission He had given them.

When you are in the middle of a storm, is your natural reaction to focus on Christ or to focus on the chaos around you? Explain.

THE GOSPEL IS CLARIFIED

GOD CALLS US TO PROCLAIM THE MESSAGE THAT SALVATION IS AVAILABLE THROUGH FAITH IN CHRIST ALONE, NOT THROUGH WORKS.

INTRODUCTION

Faith is often a common theme in pop-culture. There are bestselling songs that tell people to "just believe," and never give up the faith you need to follow your dreams. There are popular books that encourage their readers to just believe in themselves in order to achieve their goals in life. And there are movies that portray their main character as only needing to have faith in order to reach their destiny. However, whatever the pop-culture medium is used, the common denominator is this: If you just believe in yourself enough, you'll be able to do wonderful things.

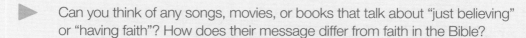 Can you think of any songs, movies, or books that talk about "just believing" or "having faith"? How does their message differ from faith in the Bible?

It's important to not just talk about faith in this generic sense, as if only having "faith" is important. Faith needs an object. Despite what pop-culture says, that object can't be ourselves or our own strength. Biblical faith isn't just about the person who believes; it's about the Person in whom we believe. It's not about having faith in a general sense, but trusting in Someone who is fully worthy of our faith. The object of our faith is what matters. It doesn't matter how much you believe if you put your faith in the wrong thing.

SETTING THE CONTEXT

Paul and Barnabas had been sent by the church at Antioch on their first missionary journey. As they traveled, they shared the gospel, planted churches, appointed leaders, and entrusted the care of these new congregations to them. All in all, it was an enormously successful trip. The gospel was flourishing among the Gentiles.

After they returned to their home base of Antioch, they celebrated with the church all that God was doing among the Gentiles. But soon they were dragged into a dispute that centered on the Jewish rite of circumcision. For centuries, circumcision was the mark that identified the people of God from the rest of the nations. Many circumcised Jews had become Christians, and some of these men came to Antioch to teach that Gentiles coming to faith in Christ must be circumcised to be saved.

A serious argument broke out regarding the nature of the gospel. Looking at "The Big Picture" (p. 70), the debate was over the requirements for redemption in Christ. The church had come to a pivotal moment, one that would not only clarify the gospel but also set the course for the expansion of the Christian witness in the future.

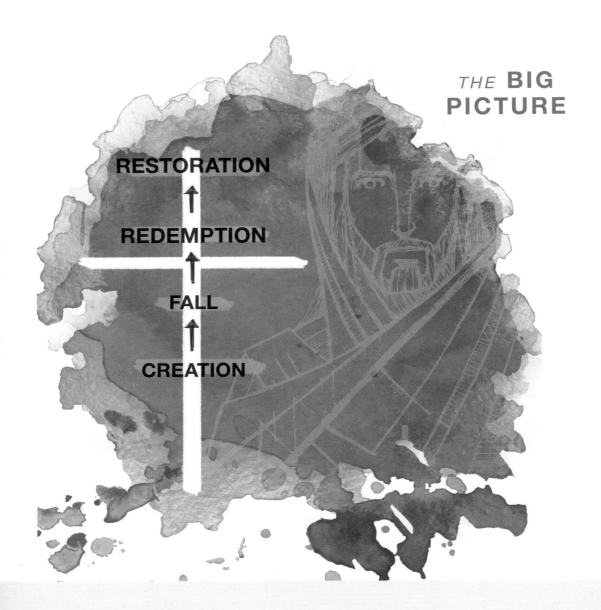

THE **BIG PICTURE**

RESTORATION

↑

REDEMPTION

↑

FALL

↑

CREATION

SESSION VIDEOS

Watch this session's video, and then continue the group discussion using the following guide.

▶ What ideas or phrases stood out to you most in the video? Why?

▶ Why is it so dangerous to add anything to the message of the gospel, as these Jewish teachers were trying to do at Antioch?

GROUP DISCUSSION

As a group, read Acts 15:1-5.

▶ How might people in the church today impose further regulation on the message of the gospel?

▶ Why do you think Paul disagreed so sharply with these teachers?

★ What was the core of the issue, if not the specific act of circumcision?

The dispute began when some men who evidently had heard the reports of Gentiles coming to faith in Christ came down from Judea to Antioch. These men did not deny the possibility of Gentiles being saved, but the possibility of anyone being saved apart from obedience to the Law. When the men arrived, they began to teach that circumcision was necessary for salvation.

When Paul and Barnabas heard what the men were teaching, they confronted them and argued about this matter with them. The whole debate can be boiled down to the question of whether Jesus alone is sufficient for salvation, or if something else—such as circumcision in this case—was needed in addition.

Paul and Barnabas rejected their teaching for at least two reasons. The primary reason concerned the core of the gospel—salvation by grace through faith alone (Eph. 2:8-9). The men from Judea were teaching that faith alone was not sufficient for salvation. They argued that a person first had to belong to God's covenant community, the people of Israel, and that becoming part of God's community required the mark of circumcision. Paul and Barnabas understood that you do not have to be part of the right people before you can be saved; anyone, anywhere can be saved the moment they trust in Jesus Christ.

Another reason Paul and Barnabas confronted the men from Judea might have been linked to their hearts as missionaries. Most missionaries engage people right where they are as they encourage people to consider the gospel. Requiring circumcision of the Gentiles would be an added burden and hindrance to the gospel.

▶ What are some issues we need to defend, like Paul and Barnabas defended the Gentiles' salvation?

As a group, read Acts 15:6-21.

▶ How would you explain Peter's argument?

⭐ Why was the Holy Spirit a critical part of this discussion?

Once again, the issue was debated for some time and then Peter stood to address the gathering and offered a strong defense of Gentiles being saved by grace alone apart from circumcision. Peter reminded the gathering of his experience with Cornelius (Acts 10–11) and how God had revealed Peter's need to set aside a mindset fixed on tradition and replace it with one fixed on the gospel.

Peter then presented God's gift of the Holy Spirit to the Gentiles as evidence of the Gentiles' conversion apart from circumcision. God had given the Gentile believers the Holy Spirit just as He had given the Holy Spirit to them. No distinction was made based on circumcision or any other factor—everyone had been saved by faith, and the giving of the Holy Spirit confirmed that God accepted that faith.

After Peter finished, the entire assembly fell completely silent. Peter's strong defense of the gospel resonated with the gathering. Paul and Barnabas then took the opportunity to echo Peter and share how God had worked through them to see Gentiles come to faith. Paul and Barnabas relayed story after story of how God had transformed the lives of many Gentiles.

Then it was James' turn. He began by affirming Peter's testimony, but then he pointed the gathering to Scripture. James quoted Amos 9:11-12 to show that the Gentiles coming to faith was part of God's plan all along. God had told their ancestors that everyone—Jews and Gentiles alike—would seek the Lord. The message of salvation had never been only for the Jews.

⭐ What is the significance of the council's decision in light of Acts 1:8?

▶ How did this decision pave the way for the future of Christian expansion?

THE KINGDOM ON EARTH

CHRIST CONNECTION

The Jerusalem Council met to resolve a dispute in the early church: Was faith in Christ sufficient for salvation and inclusion into God's family or was something else needed? The early church's response affirmed the sufficiency of faith in Jesus for salvation. Because of His finished work on the cross, Jesus alone is all we need to be saved.

OUR MISSION

◯ Head

Why is the doctrine of faith alone in Christ alone and not works so important?

What can we learn from the way the early church addressed controversy that applies to how we address controversy today?

♥ Heart

Why is it important for us to stress that purity flows from faith rather than preceding faith?

What are some other ways our lives demonstrate a genuine faith in Christ?

✋ Hands

What are some beliefs and traditions we hold onto that may interfere with others understanding the gospel?

How should the truth that salvation is by grace rather than works change the way we live?

PERSONAL STUDY: DAY 1

⭐ **The point: Despite what others may say, Christ alone is enough for salvation.**

▶ Read Acts 15:1-5.

What did the men say was at stake if people didn't obey Moses' customs?

List some similar things people believe are required for a person to be saved. What actually has to happen?

How did the church at Antioch decide to handle this issue? Was the church in Jerusalem in agreement on the issue?

The issue of being saved apart from the Law was still causing trouble throughout the region. The church leaders needed to discuss: How did Jesus' earthly ministry change things for God's people? Why are we no longer required to observe Jewish sacrifices and traditional practices?

Why is it important for you personally to be clear on what is necessary and what is not necessary for salvation?

▶ Respond

Ask yourself: Am I tempted to think there is something other than Jesus that I need in order to be considered righteous before God? Confess this to God and ask for forgiveness. Ask Him to show you the full extent of the gift Jesus gave you through the cross.

⭐ **The point: God cleanses our hearts through faith.**

▶ Read Acts 15:6-11.

The _____ and the _____ got together to talk through this issue.

Highlight the phrase "much debate" (v. 7). What does this tell you about the attention the leaders gave to this issue? How does this help us learn to handle divisions and issues within the church today?

Note who sent Peter to the Gentiles. Why was it important for Peter to acknowledge this? How did this relate to the current issue?

What did God give the Gentiles? What does this prove about the Gentiles and their place among God's chosen people?

▶ Respond

Have you ever looked at a person or group of people and thought, "They could never be saved"? Ask God to give you hope for all people to come to Him. Then pray for the salvation of that person or group of people.

When are you tempted to view traditions as equally or more important than the truth of the gospel?

PERSONAL STUDY: DAY 3

⭐ **The point: James agreed with Peter and spoke about the way that God offered salvation for the Gentiles.**

What happens when God's people argue? What changes when they support each other in sharing the truth of the gospel?

▶ Read Acts 15:12-18.

What evidence did Barnabas and Paul bring up to support Peter's remarks that God includes the Gentiles in salvation through Jesus?

James also offered his support. What was his attitude as he spoke?

▶ Read Isaiah 45:22.

Who is called to turn to the Lord and be saved? Why was this difficult for people in Paul's day to understand? Why do you think it's still difficult for people to understand today?

What does this prophecy from long ago reveal about God's plan for all people?

▶ Respond

Ask the Holy Spirit to guide you as you examine your heart. Do you have any assumptions about what a Christ-follower should look like and how they should act based on your personal preferences instead of Scripture?

What keeps you from embracing the global nature of the mission God has given you? Ask God to humble you and show you in what areas you may hold prejudices.

⭐ **The point: James encouraged the church to write a letter to the new Gentile believers to teach them, rather than causing difficulties for them.**

▶ Read Acts 15:19-21.

Why would it be important not to cause difficulties for the Gentile believers?

What did James say the Gentiles should abstain from (v. 20)?

What might be some consequences of a new believer's witness to outsiders if these rules were not obeyed?

What benefits come from writing down a decision and sending it out versus having a messenger verbally deliver the message?

▶ Respond

Do any of the commands in the Bible seem too difficult? Consider the reasons these commands exist and how they could promote unity and selfless living.

If you need help understanding why some of the commands in the Bible exist, ask a trusted church leader to help you think through these commands.

PERSONAL STUDY: DAY 5

⭐ **The point: The church decided on freedom and love for their Gentile brothers and sisters.**

▶ Read Acts 15:22-29.

Highlight the phrase "brothers and sisters among the Gentiles" (v. 23). What is the meaning of calling someone a brother or sister?

How do you think the Gentile believers responded to these titles? How do they affect you?

The _____ church decided to send Barnabas, Paul, Judas, and Silas to deliver the letter. Why is this important?

Whose decision was it not to place extra burdens on the Gentile believers? Why is it important for us to also refrain from placing requirements on new believers that are not in the Bible?

▶ Respond

Consider your friends at church. Do you notice anyone feeling like an outsider? What can you do to make them feel included?

Do you view others in your church as brothers and sisters? How can your actions reflect this knowledge of your relationship to them in Christ? List two actions you will take this week to show love to some of your brothers and sisters in Christ.

THE KING RETURNS

*GOD CALLS US TO LIVE IN LIGHT OF HIS PROMISE
TO MAKE ALL THINGS NEW.*

INTRODUCTION

Revelation is a book about the true, lasting hope we have in Christ Jesus. While there are some chilling scenes and images in the book, they are not the focus. We cannot discount God's coming judgment on the world, but ultimately Revelation is not about that. Revelation is about Jesus' return. Jesus is victorious in the end, and so are we. Jesus will return to make all things new. He will wipe away every tear from every eye, and He will put death to death once and for all. And we will be with Him forever.

 What do you long for most when you think of eternity?

Because all things are broken, all things need to be unbroken by our victorious God. Sin has ravaged creation, separating us from God and introducing chaos into a once-ordered world. But it will not stay this way. God, the good Judge, will punish evildoers and He will reward His Son—the only innocent person to ever live. And through Jesus' innocence and His sacrifice on the cross, we will stand with Him, pardoned by our divine Judge. God loves His people, and He sent Jesus to show us that. God did not leave us in our sin but ensured that we spend eternity with Him—which has been His plan all along. That is the story of Revelation. That is the story of Jesus. That is the gospel.

SETTING THE CONTEXT

The apostle John became a great apologist for the church, writing and preaching about the identity of Jesus, for which he was persecuted. As an old man he was exiled to the island of Patmos, where he received the vision we know as the Book of Revelation. God showed John a heavenly perspective on how God's story of redemption on earth would eventually come to an end with the return of Jesus Christ as the King of the universe, recognized by people from every tribe, language, people, and nation—the goal of "The Gospel Mission" (p. ??). When Jesus returns, He will make all things new, and with this new "In the beginning…" all of God's people will live forevermore in their resurrected bodies with our resurrected and reigning Savior.

THE **GOSPEL** MISSION

GROUPS	OLD TESTAMENT	THE CHURCH	NEW CREATION
TRIBE	The Twelve Tribes of Israel (Gen. 49:28; 2 Sam. 5:1)	James Wrote to "the Twelve Tribes" of Believers, Both Jew and Gentile (Jas. 1:1)	The Redeemed of God Through the Blood of the Lamb, Jesus Christ, Will Come from Every Tribe, Language, People, and Nation (Rev. 5:9-10; 7:1-17)
LANGUAGE	Languages Confused at the Tower of Babylon (Gen. 11:7-9)	By the Spirit, the Disciples Preached the Gospel in Different Languages (Acts 2)	
PEOPLE & NATION	The Different Family Lines and Kingdoms upon the Earth (Ps. 67)	A Holy Nation, a People for God's Possession (1 Pet. 2:9-10)	

"Jesus came near and said to them, 'All authority has been given to me in heaven and on earth. Go, therefore, and make disciples of all nations, baptizing them in the name of the Father and of the Son and of the Holy Spirit, teaching them to observe everything I have commanded you. And remember, I am with you always, to the end of the age.'" (Matt. 28:18-20)

SESSION VIDEOS

Watch this session's video, and then continue the group discussion using the following guide.

▶ What ideas or phrases stood out to you most in the video? Why?

▶ Why do you think so many people are fascinated by the Book of Revelation?

GROUP DISCUSSION

As a group, read Revelation 19:11-16.

⭐ What names did John use to describe Jesus? What do these names for Jesus tell us about Him?

▶ What do the descriptions of Jesus in this passage tell us about the results of His second coming?

The Rider's name is Faithful and True. Jesus never fails, and He is consistent in character. He comes to judge the earth precisely because He is faithful and true to God's will and His character. Furthermore, He is beyond our total understanding and is the ultimate Ruler. Together, these names tell us that Jesus is above all and that His majesty is beyond our comprehension.

As a group, read Revelation 21:1-5.

▶ How would you summarize the message communicated by these images?

⭐ Why is it significant that the Scripture emphasizes newness throughout this description of heaven?

As we saw at the very beginning of this series during our studies in Genesis in Volume 1, humanity is created in the image of God. Of course, it is true that we are actually far from being God, but we still reflect Him. As we come to the end of our study of the Book of Revelation, we see how God is making all things new and restoring us to a full, image-bearing relationship with Him.

As you may also remember from our study of Genesis, Eve and her husband traded eternal freedom for the bondage found in that piece of fruit. Satan deceived them into believing a lie, and as a result they rebelled against God's commands. The consequences were brokenness: broken relationships between humanity and the rest of creation, broken relationships between each other, and worst of all, a broken relationship with God. Only through a perfect man—the Messiah—could the image of God and the brokenness of humanity be redeemed and restored. That Messiah King will one day rule over the earth as Adam and Eve were supposed to (Jer. 3:5; Zech 9:9-13).

GROUP DISCUSSION *CONT.*

God has been on a mission ever since to restore and remake what was lost in the garden. This is what he promised to do after Adam and Eve fell, and it is what we have seen Him do throughout the Old Testament and into the New. By understanding the past—the sin of Adam and Eve; the incarnation of God's Son; Jesus' perfect life, death, and resurrection; as well as His ascension to the throne of the universe and the sending of the Holy Spirit to us—we can understand how and why God is renewing all things. More than that, we understand why it is important to live in light of eternity now. All things are broken, but one day God will make all things new.

> How have you experienced the consequences of a broken world in your life?

As a group, read Revelation 22:1-5.

How do these images connect with the garden of Eden described in Genesis 2? What is the significance of those connections?

Based on what you've read in Revelation 21 and 22, what are some truths about heaven you can confidently declare?

Jesus prayed for God's will to be done "on earth as it is in heaven" (Matt. 6:11). In Eden, this was a reality. God walked among His people. There was no barrier between them. Though sin broke that bond, Jesus stepped into human history to fix it. So when He prayed for heaven and earth to meet, He was not being poetic—He was proclaiming something universe-altering. He was praying for the beginning of Revelation 21–22, where Satan and sin have been defeated and God's people dwell with Him again.

Our hope is not that we escape earth altogether one day and live somewhere in heaven. We were not designed for that; we were designed to live here, on earth. But not the way we currently experience it. We were supposed to live in a place where heaven and earth are fused together. If we were sent out of the world forever, it would mean Satan won at least a partial victory and that God failed and had to come up with a Plan B. But God is sovereign and good, and He works out all things for His glory and our good (Rom. 8:28). The perfection of Eden will be restored one day, only it will be even better—the world will look like it was supposed to, covered in image-bearers who bask in the rays of God's glory for eternity. This is not something to fear; it's something to rejoice in.

And with that, the story has come full circle. What began with God creating everything good—and humanity at the pinnacle of creation ruling under His sovereignty, enjoying relationship with Him and one another, and enjoying rhythms of work and rest for His glory—has ended the same way. Well, nearly the same way—the ending is much better than the beginning.

CHRIST CONNECTION

This present age will come to an end when Christ returns to fulfill His promises and reign with His people for all eternity. The relationship lost in the garden when Adam sinned will be gloriously restored when the garden city of the New Jerusalem is unveiled and Jesus wipes away every tear from every eye. The way to be part of God's new world is to be cleansed by the blood of the Lamb, shed for our redemption.

OUR MISSION

◯ Head

How does the gospel provide comfort and understanding when it comes to dealing with the reality of death?

What do you imagine living on the new earth will be like?

♥ Heart

What are some ways we should reflect the image of God in our communities, schools, homes, and so on?

How should the future resurrection in Christ give us hope in facing the challenges of life today?

✋ Hands

How does the reality of Jesus' future restoration of all things impact the way you conduct your relationships with other people today?

Now that you have gone through the storyline of the Bible, who will you share it with this week?

PERSONAL STUDY: DAY 1

⭐ **The point: John received the words of Revelation through a vision from Jesus.**

▶ Read Revelation 1:1-3.

Verse 1 recorded how John received the Book of Revelation. Fill in the blanks to describe what happened:

The revelation was of _____ _____.

_____ gave the revelation.

He sent the angel to _____.

Underline the reason Jesus gave John this vision.

Now, rewrite verse 1 in your own words as if you were telling a friend how and why John received Revelation.

Seven blessings are listed throughout the Book of Revelation. The first one is found in verse 3. What three actions are described as "blessed"?

▶ Respond

Revelation declared the end times "must soon take place" and that the time of Jesus' return "is near." List three ways you should daily live your life based on the knowledge that Jesus could return at any time.

PERSONAL STUDY: DAY 2

⭐ **The point: As the Bride of Christ, believers prepare themselves for Christ's return.**

▶ Read Revelation 19:7-8.

What event was mentioned in this passage?

Who is the bride? Describe what she is wearing and what her clothing represents.

Highlight the three things people are called to do. Why? Explain.

Look closely at the words "his bride has prepared herself" (v. 7) and that "she was given fine linen to wear" (v. 8). We can't make ourselves pure enough for the Lamb; however, He gave us His own righteousness, His "fine linens."

What role does He play in preparing us for His return?

How can we also be ready for His return? *(Hint: Read Matt. 25:13; Rom. 10:9; 1 John 2:28.)*

▶ Respond

When you think of Christ's return, do you consider yourself glad and joyful? Fearful and unprepared? Explain.

Praying, reading your bible, spending time with other believers, and watching for opportunities to share the gospel with those around you are all ways to prepare for Christ's return. From this list, which is easiest for you? Which is most challenging? Thank God for His faithfulness in your life and ask him to help you in the areas that are more difficult as you prepare for His return.

PERSONAL STUDY: DAY 3

⭐ ## The point: When Jesus returns, He will make all things new.

▶ ### Read Revelation 21:1-5.

Highlight all the things John saw. Use another color to highlight everything he heard.

Put yourself in John's place for a moment. How would you respond if you saw and heard these things?

What promises do you see in this passage? How do these promises encourage you?

▶ ### Respond

When you think about all the sin and evil that is in the world right now, what do you most look forward to that Jesus will make right?

When we are in the middle of suffering, we sometimes forget Jesus will one day make everything right again. What difficult circumstances are you facing right now? Talk to the Lord about whatever comes to your mind and thank Him for the promises in this passage.

Memorize today's Scripture. Then, when difficult days come, you can hold on to this truth.

PERSONAL STUDY: DAY 4

⭐ **The point: When Christ returns, He will separate believers from unbelievers.**

▶ **Read Revelation 21:6-8.**

Who is speaking here? What name does He call Himself? What does that mean?

Explain the difference between those who conquer and the people mentioned in verse 8. What happens to each of these?

"Look, I am coming soon, and my reward is with me to repay each person according to his work." —Revelation 22:12

▶ **Read Revelation 22:8-15.**

In your own words, explain what John did when he heard and saw these things. What did the angel tell John to do instead?

Explain how believers and unbelievers were separated in this passage.

How should these passages motivate Christians to share the gospel?

▶ **Respond**

Death is something everyone will face, even though most don't like to think about it. Ask yourself: How does thinking about what happens to believers and unbelievers at death motivate me to share the gospel with others?

PERSONAL STUDY: DAY 5

⭐ **The point: When Christ returns, God's people will be in God's place under God's rule forever.**

▶ Read Revelation 22:1-5.

List everything the angel showed John in these verses.

What single word would you use to describe this picture?

What are some elements of the world now that will be taken away in the new world?

Why is there no need for lamps or sun?

Highlight the phrases in this passage that bring the most encouragement to you.

▶ Respond

Take some time to reflect on everything this passage offers to those who give their life to Christ. How does this future promise compare to any short-term benefits of sin?

Write a prayer of gratitude to the Lord, thanking Him for His creation, His perfect plan of redemption, the life He's given you in Christ, and the promise of His return.

HOW TO USE THE LEADER GUIDE

Prepare to Lead

The Leader Guide is designed to be cut out along the dotted line so you, the leader, can have this front-and-back page with you as you lead your group through the session.

Watch the session video and *read through the session content* with the Leader Guide cut-out in hand and notice how it supplements each section of the study.

Use the *Session Objective* in the Leader Guide to help focus your preparation and leadership in the group session.

Questions & Answers

⭐ Questions in the session content with this icon have some sample answers provided in the Leader Guide, if needed, to help you jump-start or steer the conversation.

Setting the Context

This section of the session always has an *infographic* on the opposite page. The Leader Guide provides an activity to help your group members interact with the content communicated through the infographic.

Group Discussion

The Group Discussion contains the main teaching content for each session, providing questions for students to interact with as you move through the biblical passages. Some of these questions will have suggested answers in the Leader Guide.

Our Mission ⭕ ✅ ✋

The Our Mission is a summary application section designed to highlight how the biblical passages being studied challenge the way we think, feel, and live today. Some of these questions will have suggested answers in the Leader Guide.

Pray

Conclude each group session with a prayer. A brief sample prayer is provided at the end of each Leader Guide cut-out.

SESSION 1 · LEADER GUIDE

Session Objective

Show how the Holy Spirit was given to fulfill God's promise and to empower the church to live for Christ and complete the mission He gave.

Introducing the Study

Use this intro to set the context for the study on Pentecost.

Setting the Context

Use the following activity to help group members see the blessing and assurance that come with the presence of the Holy Spirit.

Direct group members to look over the connections on "Hearing the Old Testament in Acts" (p. 10). Ask them to identify how these connections relate to the stories and promises of the Bible that have been covered in this study. Then ask: "How are you encouraged by the fact that God's plan foretold in the Old Testament included the coming of the Holy Spirit and the existence of the church, of which you are a part as a believer in Christ?"

Read this paragraph to transition to the next part of the study:

Just as Jesus' crucifixion and resurrection were not God's Plan B, neither was the coming of the Holy Spirit and formation of the church, with all her variety of people and gifts. God's Plan A, from before time and foretold in the Old Testament, includes us as believers in Christ, filled with the Spirit, gathered with the church, and living on mission for Jesus' name.

Group Discussion

Watch this session's video, and then as part of the group discussion, use these answers as needed for the questions highlighted in this section.

⭐ How does this passage reveal both the power and the purpose of the Holy Spirit? *1) The power of the Holy Spirit is illustrated by the elements of wind and fire, both of which have the power to move and reshape God's creation. 2) The purpose of the Holy Spirit is to come upon believers individually in Jesus Christ to empower them or the mission and to assure them of Christ's presence. 3) The Holy Spirit empowers believers for communicating the gospel.*

⭐ Why is it important that Peter gave the people a way to respond? *1) The gospel must be heard so people can believe, but if there is no repentance and faith in response to the gospel, then people remain dead in their sins. 2) Conviction of sin does not equate to knowing how to respond in faith, so sharing the gospel should involve a clear statement of response. 3) Peter's instruction to the crowd helps us know how to respond to the gospel and how to lead others to respond to the gospel.*

⭐ What does it mean that the early church was filled with awe of God? How might this relate to "the fear of the Lord"? *1) The work of God in the salvation of sinners is a wonder to behold. 2) "The fear of the Lord" refers to a deep reverence for our Creator and Savior; we dare not come to Him lightly, but we can come to Him in confidence. 3) The fear of the Lord should lead to faith-filled obedience, acknowledging God's holiness and justice and rejoicing in His love, mercy, and grace.*

Our Mission

✔ How should the indwelling of the Spirit change the way believers live? *This account in Acts 2 challenges the way we thing about sharing the gospel. Many people struggle to speak up, know when to share their faith, or start conversations about Jesus. Different techniques are often suggested for making those conversations easier. In fact, many churches offer whole classes on the subject, and that's not a bad thing at all. But at its most basic level, maybe the easiest way to become bold in sharing the gospel is by seeking to be filled with the Spirit.*

Pray

Close your group in prayer, thanking God for the gift of the Holy Spirit and asking Him to motivate you to give yourself fully to His mission.

SESSION 2 · LEADER GUIDE

Session Objective

Show that persecution of the early church began from within Israel, resulting in the spread of the gospel and the strengthening of the church.

Introducing the Study

Use this option as an introduction to talk about dealing with persecution in light of the glory and joy that await believers for eternity.

Setting the Context

Use the following activity to help group members see the power of faithful suffering for the name of Jesus.

Instruct your group to look at "Suffering for Jesus" (p. 22). Ask them to point out any parallels they see between the suffering in the early church and the suffering Jesus experienced (arrested, prayer, healings, tried and flogged by the Sanhedrin, continued faithfulness, wonders and signs, false accusations, death outside the city, prayer for forgiveness). Then ask the following questions: "Why do you think there are so many parallels in the suffering between the early church and Jesus?" "How is it possible to rejoice for being counted worthy to suffer for Jesus' name?" "What must the early church have believed about God the Father, God the Son, and God the Holy Spirit to have endured and rejoiced in suffering for Jesus' name?"

Group Discussion

Watch this session's video, and then as part of the group discussion, use these answers as needed for the questions highlighted in this section.

⭐ What attributes of Stephen are evident from these verses? *1) He was filled with the Holy Spirit. 2) He was full of grace and power by the Spirit, performing miracles among the people. 3) He spoke with wisdom and truth by the Spirit as he debated with those who opposed him.*

⭐ What does Stephen's use of Scripture reveal about how he viewed it? *1) Stephen believed Scripture was true and trustworthy. 2) Stephen believed the stories of Scripture had meaning and purpose that could be applied to life. 3) Stephen believed the Scriptures ability to convict the human heart of sin.*

⭐ What was the purpose of Stephen's vision of Jesus standing next to God's throne? *1) Stephen's vision of Jesus standing in heaven affirmed the quality of his testimony to the gospel of Jesus. 2) Jesus is typically referred to as seated in heaven, ruling over creation, so His standing shows great honor for Stephen. 3) Jesus takes interest in the lives of His witnesses, and this vision is a reminder that Jesus is indeed with them to the end of the age.*

Our Mission

⭕ How have you seen Christians be falsely accused? *As the culture around us becomes more hostile to Christianity and a Christian worldview, we shouldn't be surprised if we experience hostility similar to Stephen's. Stephen was accused of speaking blasphemy against the temple. In our case, it's more likely that we'll be accused of hateful speech, bias, and intolerance, simply because we hold to biblical beliefs about the value of human life, the meaning of marriage, and the origins of sexuality.*

🔽 Why do you think people respond better to a humble person than an arrogant one? *Stephen didn't let the fact that he was right make him judgmental or arrogant in his speech. He may have had some harsh rebukes for the religious leaders, but as he died, he cried out for God not to hold their actions against them. Like Jesus, he asked for mercy for his persecutors. His actions were not motivated by pride—an eagerness to be right and to prove his rightness—but by love. He wanted them to believe in Jesus, not simply to give him the argument. Preaching, evangelizing, and defending the faith must come from a heart of love and compassion for the lost, not from an ego that simply wants to win.*

Pray

Close your group in prayer, asking that you would have the courage and conviction to stand for the gospel even if it is costly.

SESSION 3 · LEADER GUIDE

Session Objective

Show how Philip brought the gospel outside of Jerusalem to Samaria and to a Gentile according to what Jesus had said in Acts 1:8. In a way, this session will lay the groundwork for the next few.

Introducing the Study

Use this section to talk about God's providence in providing opportunities for the message of Christ to spread.

Setting the Context

Use the following activity to help group members see how the gospel spread just as Jesus said it would.

Note on "Expansion of the Early Church in Palestine" (p. 34) that Jesus' disciples were to begin their mission in Jerusalem and spread out to Judea and Samaria. Remind the group once again that persecution was the catalyst for the disciples leaving Jerusalem to fulfill this next step of the mission. Then ask the following questions:

• What are some ways the ministry of the disciples echoes that of Jesus? *Philip preached in Samaria like Jesus; Peter healed a paralytic like Jesus; Stephen died outside Jerusalem like Jesus; Peter raised a little girl to life like Jesus.*

• What are some similarities and differences between the mission efforts on this map and Joshua's mission of conquering the promised land? *Both the disciples and Joshua and the Israelites traveled north and south to fulfill their missions; Joshua was sent in to destroy people and drive them out on account of their sin, but the disciples were sent to share the message of Jesus in order to save people from their sin; both Joshua and the disciples experienced miraculous orders and success.*

Group Discussion

Watch this session's video, and then as part of the group discussion, use these answers as needed for the questions highlighted in this section.

⭐ How would you describe Philip's response to the Spirit's instructions? What does this tell us about Philip? *1) Philip was quick to obey, even with vague and open-ended instructions. 2) Philip was bold to approach someone whom he had never met. 3) Philip was filled with the Holy Spirit, humble, and passionate about sharing the gospel.*

⭐ What can we learn from Philip's approach to sharing the gospel? *1) Be obedient, even when God's instructions take you outside of your comfort zone. 2) Devote yourself to the apostles' teaching—God's Word—so you can answer questions from unbelievers with both knowledge and faith. 3) Trust the Holy Spirit for direction and words when sharing the gospel with an unbeliever.*

⭐ What did the man's question in verse 36 reveal? How does this reflect a changed heart? *1) That he believed the message about Jesus. 2) That he wanted to respond with an act of obedience—baptism. 3) The heart of a believer wants to obey the commands of Jesus.*

Our Mission

🔻 How can we cultivate hearts willing to respond obediently to the Spirit's leading, no matter the risks? *When we think about sharing the gospel with a lost world, we often focus on the hostility and resistance Christians experience. However, resistance and hostility aren't always the reactions to the gospel. The story of the Ethiopian reminds us that many are seeking God as a result of God first seeking them. In this case, the Ethiopian knew enough to come to Jerusalem to look for Him, but in many cases, people will look wherever some semblance of hope and spirituality can be found.*

Pray

Close your group in prayer, asking that you and your group would be obedient to the leading of the Holy Spirit for opportunities to share the gospel.

SESSION 4 · LEADER GUIDE

Session Objective

Show how God was at work to save even the most unlikely of people in Saul and how he was given the task of advancing the gospel to the Gentiles. This connects back to the previous session, where we saw Philip share with one Gentile, and with the next session, where we see Saul and Barnabas sent on mission.

Introducing the Study

Use this option to set the context for Saul's conversion.

Setting the Context

Use the following activity to help group members see the power of God in a life changed by encountering Jesus.

Direct your group to review the timeline of "Paul's Life" (p. 46). Explain that Paul saw himself as an example of the extreme reach of God's patience and grace—if God could save him, He can save anyone (1 Tim. 1:12-17). Then ask the following questions:

• In what sense are we all like Paul, the worst of sinners (1 Tim. 1:15)? *We all stand condemned before God on account of our sin, from the persecutor to the people-pleaser.*

• What is the only difference between Paul "the Christian" and Paul "the Missionary"? *Paul and Barnabas were set apart by the Holy Spirit for their missionary calling; otherwise, Paul preached and taught everywhere he was, whether in his local context or on the mission field.*

Group Discussion

Watch this session's video, and then as part of the group discussion, use these answers as needed for the questions highlighted in this section.

⭐ What might Jesus have wanted to teach Saul through his blindness? *1) That Saul had been blind to the true nature and heart of God. 2) That true sight comes from faith in Jesus, experienced in the community of the church. 3) That truly Jesus is the One who gives sight to the blind.*

⭐ What does God's plan for Saul reveal about His power and purposes? *1) God has the power to change anyone's heart, even an enemy of the faith. 2) God has His plans and purposes for people before they even come to faith in Jesus. 3) Everyone God saves has the purpose of being a witness for Jesus wherever they are.*

⭐ What is significant about the way Ananias addressed Saul? *1) Saul was no longer an enemy of God but a member of God's family in Christ. 2) Saul was no longer a persecutor of the church but a brother in the faith with those whom he had come to imprison. 3) Though temporarily blinded by the experience with Jesus, Saul was now a believer with a changed heart, mind, perspective, and purpose.*

Our Mission

⭕ How does Saul's story of conversion deepen your own gratitude for God's grace and mercy? *As in the parable of the Prodigal Son (Luke 15:11-32), the challenge here is not for the self-indulgent, wandering younger brother who rejected his father, left home, and wasted his inheritance. Instead, the challenge is for the self-righteous older brother who stayed home and worked diligently for his father, believing he had earned his father's love. Saul was like the older brother because he also sincerely believed he was obeying and pleasing God.*

🔽 God used a unique collision with Saul to get his attention. In what ways do you see Jesus "colliding" with people today? *Jesus doesn't collide with us to produce superficial, religious obedience. Saul excelled in that before his encounter with Jesus. Jesus meets with us to show us who He is and to transform our hearts, leading to loving, genuine obedience. Jesus' encounter with Saul shows that He can soften the hardest hearts, even the hearts of people who are full of themselves.*

Pray

Close your group in prayer, asking that you would be confident in the power of the gospel and motivated to share boldly the good news of Jesus with the world.

SESSION 5 · LEADER GUIDE

Session Objective

Show how God's chosen method of taking the gospel to all the world is missionaries, while also emphasizing that we are all to live on mission in our context.

Introducing the Study

Use this intro to discuss the context of the church's first missionaries.

Setting the Context

Use the following activity to help group members see the strength and boldness that are available through the Holy Spirit in the lives of believers.

Draw attention to the map "The First Missionary Journey of Paul" (p. 58). Ask the group to describe the theme for Paul's stops on the mainland (opposition; dangerous). Then ask the following questions: "Why do you think Paul and Barnabas faced such opposition in these cities?" "What temptations might they have faced in light of the opposition and danger for preaching the gospel?" "What can we know about their faith given that they retraced their steps through those same cities before returning home?"

Read this paragraph to transition to the next part of the study:

Surely Paul and Barnabas considered giving up and going home, or maybe they thought about lessening the intensity of the gospel message. But they did neither. They remained faithful to go where God led them and to say what God wanted them to say. They remained faithful, and that was good and right.

Group Discussion

Watch this session's video, and then as part of the group discussion, use these answers as needed for the questions highlighted in this section.

⭐ How would you describe the priorities of the church at Antioch based on these verses? *1) To be a church for all the nations. 2) To be a church focused on and devoted to God and His will. 3) To be a church that lived by faith.*

⭐ How would you describe the missionaries' ministry philosophy based on these verses? *1) First to the Jew, then to the Gentile. 2) They shared the gospel like scattering seed; they proclaimed the message about Jesus and then moved on to another town. 3) They shared the gospel in public settings and by request with individuals.*

⭐ What purpose did the miracle of judgment serve in this passage? *1) The miracle of judgment served to back up the missionaries' gospel message. 2) Elymas's blindness demonstrated that his brand of religion as a Jewish false prophet was also blind, like Paul's experience after his encounter with Jesus. 3) This miracle showed the Gentile proconsul that the missionaries worshiped the one true God, and he believed.*

Our Mission

○ How do you see yourself—through what you do or who God has made you to be in Christ? *Paul and Barnabas took on an identity as being sent by God away from their home for the purpose of helping others discover their Christ-given identity (Acts 13:2). We also have this compelling identity. This is why we make disciples. This is why we "go" wherever we are. The good news of the gospel we believe pushes us to go and help others believe it too. We are disciples of Jesus sent to make disciples with Jesus among our neighbors and the nations.*

✋ How are you making disciples of Jesus wherever you are? *The God who sends continues to call us to share His heart for unreached people and to send more missionaries around the world. If we want to be faithful to His calling, we need to personalize this sending. We must each ask ourselves: Where is God sending me as a missionary? If God's answer is that we should stay where we are, then we ask how we will support those who have been sent.*

Pray

Close your group in prayer, praying that you and your church would prioritize the mission of God appropriately.

SESSION 6 · LEADER GUIDE

Session Objective

Show how the early church settled a vital dispute over the nature of salvation, which protected the gospel message that continued to be carried forth and also established a pattern of how the church should settle disputes. This session needs to have a broad view of the rest of the church age, perhaps covering in the conclusion how the early church continued to carry this gospel message forward on two more missionary journeys by Paul and that it continues to hold the church together today.

Introducing the Study

Use this option to discuss the early church's emphasis upon grace alone, by faith alone, through Christ alone as the basis of salvation.

Setting the Context

Use the following activity to help group members see the importance of understanding the storyline of the Bible.

Ask your group to look at "The Big Picture" (p. 70). Explain that this summarizes the storyline of the Bible we have been studying. Allow your group members a couple of moments to comment on these headings, sharing details of the Bible stories they remember, explaining how the phases relate to one another, etc. Then ask this question:

• How does the nature of the fall set up the requirements for redemption? *The fall came as the result of a prideful heart that wanted to be like God, and this sinful nature has been passed on to us all. Sin is more than just an external act; it is the fruit of a sinful heart. So redemption cannot come from external acts but only from a heart change.*

Group Discussion

Watch this session's video, and then as part of the group discussion, use these answers as needed for the questions highlighted in this section.

⭐ What was the core of the issue, if not the specific act of circumcision? *1) It was preserving the heritage of the Jews. 2) It was the jealousy of the older brother from Jesus' parable; they refused to celebrate the simple repentance of Gentile converts. 3) These Jewish teachers still believed they could find salvation through keeping the law.*

⭐ Why was the Holy Spirit a critical part of this discussion? *1) The Father and the Son freely give the gift of the Holy Spirit to all who believe in Jesus' name. 2) If the Gentile believers received the Holy Spirit apart from taking on circumcision, then it must not be required for salvation. 3) The Holy Spirit is the down payment, the proof of our salvation, not circumcision.*

⭐ What is the significance of the council's decision in light of Acts 1:8? *1) The gospel witness could continue unhindered among the Gentiles. 2) The Christians were to be Jesus' witnesses in the world, not witnesses for the law of Moses. 3) The few expectations for the Gentiles were to enable the gospel to be shared without hindrance by Gentile believers with Jewish unbelievers.*

Our Mission

What can we learn from the way the early church addressed controversy that applies to how we address controversy today? *The way the Jerusalem Council handled the dispute surrounding circumcision in Acts 15 is an example for how we should handle disputes in the church today. We address disagreements as they arise, appeal to Scripture and what God has done, and call for freedom in Christ and love to guide how we all live together after the issue has been resolved. The Jerusalem Council also emphasized the sufficiency of faith in Jesus for salvation and inclusion into God's family by stating that He alone is all we need for salvation. The early church protected the core message of the gospel.*

Why is it important for us to stress that purity flows from faith rather than preceding faith? *Circumcision had been a mark of purity and separateness from the world for God's people. Now, in Christ, that mark comes by faith. In Christ, purity and separateness do not lead into salvation, but instead flow out of it. Requiring circumcision before salvation undermined this essential aspect of the gospel. As the apostle Paul would say elsewhere, those who follow Christ experience a circumcision of the heart when they put off the old self and take up the new (Rom. 2:28-29). It is the inner life of faith in Christ that is important, not a ritual act.*

Pray

Close your group in prayer, thanking God for the simple truth of the gospel and praying that you would be able to keep that truth unpolluted.

SESSION 7 · LEADER GUIDE

Session Objective

Show how the gospel story ends with Jesus' return and all things being made new, all of the consequences of sin being dealt with, and us enjoying eternal, unhindered relationship with God as He intended. We should stress that this is our hope and the fullness of the gospel—it does not end with our personal salvation; we are still growing in the gospel as we continue to look forward to this day.

Introducing the Study

Use this section to introduce the book of Revelation and the future that awaits all of humanity.

Setting the Context

Use the following activity to help group members see the purpose and the result of the gospel mission we have received.

Direct your group to read over "The Gospel Mission" (p. 82). Ask the group to identify ways the gospel mission of the church picks up on themes that have been communicated through the storyline of Scripture (God's heart for the nations; reconciliation among the peoples; all praise and glory to the Son for His obedience to the cross and resurrection). Then ask the following questions: "How has the storyline of Scripture helped you to better understand the identity and work of Jesus?" "How have you been encouraged to live on mission in light of the Bible's storyline?"

Read this paragraph to transition to the next part of the study:

The storyline of Scripture helps make sense of the various stories of the Bible, but even further, it helps us see the importance of Jesus' coming and second coming and challenges us to obey Jesus and live on mission for the sake of His great name. Let us not miss the point of Scripture; let us point everyone to Jesus just as the Bible does.

Group Discussion

Watch this session's video, and then as part of the group discussion, use these answers as needed for the questions highlighted in this section.

⭐ What names did John use to describe Jesus? What do these names for Jesus tell us about Him? *1) Faithful and True: Jesus is trustworthy, faithful, and always keeps His promises. 2) The Word of God: Jesus communicates and acts in complete alignment with God because He is God. His Word is powerful and never fails. 3) King of Kings and Lord of Lords: Jesus' rule is supreme over all other kings, lords, rulers, and authorities. Everyone will bow to Him.*

⭐ Why is it significant that the Scripture emphasizes newness throughout this description of heaven? *1) The current heavens and earth are marred by sin and awaiting redemption. 2) The Christian looks forward to the second coming of Jesus in part because of the promise of the resurrection to new bodies free from sin and death. 3) God has promised since the beginning that the serpent will be crushed by His Son, and this will entail a new beginning free from temptation and sin.*

⭐ How do these images connect with the garden of Eden described in Genesis 2? What is the significance of those connections? *1) The tree of life is available to all believers in the new heavens and new earth, so eternal life is guaranteed. 2) There will no longer be any curse; the work of human beings will again be joyful and completely God-glorifying as we obey God with our whole hearts. 3) God's presence is once again with humanity in His fullness, unhindered by sin and never to be lost again.*

Our Mission

✋ How does the reality of Jesus' future restoration of all things impact the way you conduct your relationships with other people today? *As we have seen, our hope rests in what Christ has done and what He will do one day. We rest secure in our salvation based on Jesus' redemptive work and, while everything continues to fall apart, we place our hope in Jesus to restore it when He returns. Until then, we don't just sit and wait—we join God's mission to continue to expand the gospel to the entire world. We take the hope that we have and share it with all who will listen.*

Pray

Close your group in prayer, thanking God for the promise that He is in control of all history and is bringing it together under the lordship of Christ.

Enjoyed *Gospel Foundations*? Check out *The Gospel Project for Students* to find out more about God's Story of Redemption.

GROUP DIRECTORY

Name: _____

Home Phone: _____

Mobile Phone: _____

Email: _____

Social Media: _____

Name: _____

Home Phone: _____

Mobile Phone: _____

Email: _____

Social Media: _____

Name: _____

Home Phone: _____

Mobile Phone: _____

Email: _____

Social Media: _____

Name: _____

Home Phone: _____

Mobile Phone: _____

Email: _____

Social Media: _____

Name: _____

Home Phone: _____

Mobile Phone: _____

Email: _____

Social Media: _____

Name: _____

Home Phone: _____

Mobile Phone: _____

Email: _____

Social Media: _____

Name: _____

Home Phone: _____

Mobile Phone: _____

Email: _____

Social Media: _____

Name: _____

Home Phone: _____

Mobile Phone: _____

Email: _____

Social Media: _____

Name: _____

Home Phone: _____

Mobile Phone: _____

Email: _____

Social Media: _____

Name: _____

Home Phone: _____

Mobile Phone: _____

Email: _____

Social Media: _____

Name: _____

Home Phone: _____

Mobile Phone: _____

Email: _____

Social Media: _____

Name: _____

Home Phone: _____

Mobile Phone: _____

Email: _____

Social Media: _____